Perfect Moments with God

Paul E. Tupper

Copyright © 2025 Paul E. Tupper

Several of the pieces in this book previously appeared in the online version of Fairfield County Catholic.

Perfect Moments Press
New York, NY

Perfect.moment2025@gmail.com

All rights reserved.

ISBN: 979-8-218-61136-1

DEDICATION

I dedicate this book to my late wife, Jean. Selfless love came naturally to her. The way Jean lived her life was an inspiration to me and the basis for many of the concepts you will read about.

CONTENTS

ACKNOWLEDGEMENTS	i
INTRODUCTION	iii

Prodigal Sons and Daughters	1
Our Spiritual GPS	4
It Just Doesn't Make Sense	7
A Light in My Darkest Hour	10
My Road to Damascus	13
Live in the Moment	17
Perfect Moments	20
What Could Possibly Be So Important?	23
Joy	26
Saying Yes	29
Doing What We Can With What We Have	32
Being Disciples	35
Paying it Forward	38
Our Reassurance	41
It's a Team Effort	44
Less is More	47
God's Schedule	50
Overwhelmed by Peace	53

Be Alert	56
I've Got This	59
Working for God	62
Our Father is Proud	65
Our Inner Circle	67
In Our Weakness	70
Walking Humbly with God	73
"I Must Decrease"	76
One of the Chosen	79
Becoming More Like Jesus	83
Recognizing Jesus	86
Behind the Scenes	89
It's Up to Us	92
Co-heirs?	95
Allowing God to Influence Us	98
Just Be Willing	101
Managing Expectations	104
It's Where You Finish	107
Listening for Jesus	110
So Grateful	113
We are Gifts	116
Be Patient	119
Our Desert Place	122
Trying too Hard	125
God's Plan	128
Stress the Positive	131

Being Close to Jesus	134
App Updates	137
Put it on the House Account	140
Our Easter Gift	142
Easter People	145
Being Thankful	148
Joy in Finding Jesus	151
My Emmaus	154
A Thank You Prayer	156
Feeling Special	158
Seek His Face	161
The Proper Perspective	163
Managing our Spiritual Lives	166
Small Seeds	169
It's Not a Check-the-Box Exercise	172
Embracing the Small Steps	175
Leading by Example	178
Our Spiritual Charger	181
The Holy Spirit – Our Enabler	184
Christ Dwelling in Us Through the Holy Spirit	187
The Holiness of the Eucharist	190
Finding the Messiah	193
Jesus' Peace	196
He Never Gives Up	198
Thank God for Moms	201
They Doubted	204

Jesus' Anger	207
Don't Blur the Lines	210
It's Not About Me	213
Returning to Work, School…and God	216
Mentors and Advocates	218
My New Boss	221
Multi-tasking with God	224
Recharge Time	227
Being Aligned	229
Keep it Simple	232
Anxiety	235
The Importance of Prayer	238
Giving God Trouble	241
Quality Time	244
God Does Not Ration the Spirit	247
Faith, Hope and Love	250
Temptations	253
Being With God in Prayer	256
In His Vortex	259
Our Christmas Gifts	262
The Magnet	265
Humility	268
Jesus' Tears	271
Chaos	274
Don't Follow the Crowd	277
No One Can Take it Away From Us	280

Things Are Not as They Seem	283
No Password Required	286
"Hold on Loosely"	288
See the Ball	291
Winning	295
Moving Forward	297
Look Up	300
The Answer Key	302
Our Secret Weapon	305
Oh Come, Let Us Adore Him	308

ABOUT THE AUTHOR	311

PAUL E. TUPPER

ACKNOWLEDGEMENTS

Writing this book was an incredibly rewarding experience. The process helped me to better understand my faith and deepen my relationship with God. On my own, I could never have done it. The topics and the words I wrote about were inspired by the Holy Spirit. Therefore, above all, I thank God for the grace and wisdom He bestowed on me.

There also are numerous individuals who provided invaluable help along the way.

My mom has had a huge impact on my faith throughout my life. When I was little she taught me how to pray. Currently, she and I have frequent conversations about theological topics. I continue to learn from her. She was such a positive influence during the writing process, always asking me to send draft reflections to her. She read every one and always provided valuable feedback.

A few years ago, God brought Jessica into my life. We initially formed a friendship based on a similar experience. What started as a friendship became love. It didn't take long for me to realize that Jessica was the person with whom I wanted to spend the rest of my life. Jessica has positively impacted not only my personal life but also my spiritual life. She encouraged me to write and, more importantly, challenged me to get my writing out in the public domain. In fact, Jessica frequently pushed me out of my comfort zone, and each time she did, I made meaningful progress on the book.

My sister Christine was the first one to tell me that I should do spiritual writing. She was convinced that my experiences might be helpful to others. Christine has been unwavering in her support for me, and her faith is rock solid. She's an inspiration to me.

I extend a special thank you to Joe Pisani. Joe has been helpful in so many ways: giving me the confidence that I could do this, providing advice along the way and getting several of my reflections published in the Fairfield County Catholic.

Joe also helped in another significant manner: He introduced me to Jim Zebora. One of the best days I had during this project was when Jim agreed to be my editor. Jim has been invaluable – not only with his editing, but in helping me to navigate the myriad of requirements necessary to get a book published. Thank you, Jim!

I also express my gratitude to Rev. Aidan Donahue of Precious Blood Parish in Milford, Conn. I approached Father Aidan early on and asked him to read some sample reflections. He graciously agreed to do so and provided me with insightful feedback. More importantly, he encouraged me to continue with my writing.

I thank Jack Fowler as well. Jack also assisted in reading some draft reflections and gave very constructive feedback which enabled my reflections to be crisper and more to the point.

Finally, I am blessed to have an amazing son, Paul Joseph. We were always a very close family, and after Jean passed, Paul and I became even closer. Because of the covid lockdown, he and I spent almost a year together, and what a blessing that year was. Paul's presence and his quiet strength were an inspiration to me and gave me strength – strength initially to grieve, strength to heal and ultimately the strength to move forward.

PAUL E. TUPPER

INTRODUCTION

This book is a compilation of short reflections that summarize my faith journey – a lifelong quest that has seen much happiness and profound grief; purposeful years but also periods of uncertainty; success and often celebration and yet, at other times, despondence. God has gotten me through it all, and these reflections tell the story. I hope my readers will find my moments with God meaningful as they seek to discern their own spiritual connection with the Almighty.

From an early age, my faith has been important to me. I was born into a devout family. We went to mass every Sunday and said grace before every meal. I prayed regularly and read the Bible often.

After college, I landed a position at a public accounting firm. It was a busy and challenging job, but I enjoyed it, so I stayed – for thirty-four years. During that time, my faith continued to be important to me, but I didn't have much free time, so I didn't do much to develop that faith beyond the aforementioned items.

I was married to an amazing person, Jean. Jean was an angel flying low. I was blessed to have her as my wife, and we had an incredible marriage that spanned 28 years. We had one child – a son named Paul who was a terrific kid and is now an even better young man. We were a small but extremely close family. Jean was the magic that made everything work.

In 2018 Jean was diagnosed with cancer. From the first day she was diagnosed, Jean and I prayed constantly that God would take the cancer away. I always knew that Jean's faith was strong, but during the year that she was sick, I saw just how amazing her faith was. She put her complete trust in God. Ultimately, God called Jean back to Him.

I was devastated and struggled to find my way. I felt like I was in a fog, literally and figuratively, for weeks. Eventually, I decided to return to my job at the accounting firm. It was a helpful distraction, and I buried myself in work. Work allowed me to escape from the reality that Jean was gone and wasn't coming back. Everything in my life seemed out of balance.

Throughout this time, Jesus gently stood beside me and ever so slightly pulled me toward Him. I didn't realize it then, but it's now easy to see with the benefit of hindsight. Over the ensuing year, Jesus patiently communicated with me. I tried to find a few moments of quiet time each day, and during those times, Jesus guided me. Eventually, I understood that He wanted me to make a major change in my life. He wanted me to work for Him. More specifically, Jesus was calling me to write.

That realization was very unsettling. For my entire adult life, I had held one job with one company. I didn't know anything else. I certainly didn't have any experience as a writer. Yet, I was certain that it's what God wanted me to do. So I retired from my job and started to write.

One of the lessons I learned in the course of this project is to slow things down. Our lives are hectic – mine was no exception – and, too often, we don't remind ourselves to take some time, shut everything else out and be in God's presence. It can make all the difference in the world.

When we make time to be in God's presence, we allow Him to share in our burdens. We realize that we don't have face our problems alone. In addition, we are able to experience the profound peace that only God can provide.

It only requires a few minutes each day. Boy, do I wish I understood that during my working days. I hope the book helps others to understand this concept sooner than I did.

I also learned to be more focused on seeing God's grace in the normal activities of life and being the source of God's grace to someone else. It's easy to miss the brilliant sunset because we have our heads buried in our phones. Similarly, if we're too focused on our problems, we may miss the opportunity to assist the elderly man struggling to carry his groceries out of the store.

Each of these experiences – the feeling of peace from being in God's presence, seeing His gift of a beautiful sunset, taking a minute to bring Christ's grace to someone not expecting it – is a perfect moment. Every minute we spend with our God is a perfect moment.

Paul E. Tupper
January 2025

PAUL E. TUPPER

PRODIGAL SONS AND DAUGHTERS

...if we return to God with a sincere heart — if we come to Him as we are, battered and worn — God will welcome us back, just as He did in the parable of the prodigal son.

It was a few days before Thanksgiving, and our son was coming home. Paul had been away at college; we hadn't seen him in months. I couldn't wait until he got home. I took the day off from work just to be there when he arrived. Our house sat on a bluff, and the front sunroom had a panoramic view. I could look all the way down the street past the harbor. I stood in that room for what seemed like hours waiting for his car to come around the bend.

Where was he? What was taking so long? I rationalized that it must be the holiday traffic that was delaying him. I paced back and forth, looking for his car. Finally, I saw a gray sedan off in the distance. As it got closer, I realized that it was Paul. My heart filled with joy as I raced to the door to meet him when he pulled up. When he got out of the car, I ran to him and threw my arms around him. I didn't want to let go. Our son was home!

Every parent has had such a moment. First, the anticipation and the unwavering hope, followed by the feeling of pure joy. We may think that these experiences are limited to parents with their young children. We might think that no one would have that same longing for us as adults. If we think that, we would be wrong.

Our heavenly Father is looking for us. He's not waiting for us to return home from college or a long trip. However, we have been away. We've strayed from Him by putting ourselves first. God made us co-heirs to His Kingdom, but we've turned our backs on Him. Like the prodigal son, we squandered our inheritance.

Thankfully, the parable of the prodigal son had a happy ending. The son eventually came to his senses and returned to his father. He expected his father to be angry. He expected to be punished, and knew he deserved whatever punishment would be doled out. He was willing to accept the role of a servant.

To the son's immense surprise, that's not what happened. Charles Martin, in his book *What If It's True*, captured the next moment vividly. His father was "still standing on the porch. Yet to leave his post." ... "Scanning the horizon. Searching for any sign of movement." Then: "Something atop the hill catches his eye." When he realizes it's his son, "The father exits the porch as if shot out of a cannon." (*What If It's True*, p.199) What an amazing image of our heavenly Father!

The same thing happens with us. Over and over we regress into our sinful nature. We waste the inheritance Jesus gave us, and we don't deserve to get it back. But if we return to God with a sincere heart – if we come to Him as we are, battered and worn – God will welcome us back, just as He did in the parable of the prodigal son.

It's not just that He will take us back. Like the father in the parable, God is actually waiting for us. Just like I couldn't wait for Paul to get home, God is looking for us, hopeful for our return. He stands watchful. He hasn't taken back the inheritance He promised. It doesn't matter what we might have done or not done. If we return to him and repent, He will immediately restore us and our place in His Kingdom.

We are prodigal sons and daughters. We have turned away from God and have put ourselves first. We've done it time and time again. But as prodigal sons and daughters, we have a Father who never stops loving us and who stands on the porch looking for us. Once we make the decision to return to Him, He will jump off and run to us, throwing His arms around us, and He won't want to let go.

July 30, 2024

OUR SPIRITUAL GPS

We have the Holy Spirit as our guide. Just like our GPS app, when we turn to Him, He will direct us.

How would we exist today without GPS apps? Like most people, I have a GPS app on my phone and use it constantly. When going somewhere for the first time, I'm totally dependent on my GPS, blindly relying on its instructions. It could be taking me 100 miles off course, and I probably wouldn't even realize it. It's hard to remember life before GPS came along.

When I was in college, I drove from Connecticut to Maryland to visit my sister. There was no GPS then. I studied the map beforehand and embarked on the trip and made it all the way to her house without a single wrong turn. It's difficult to imagine doing that now! When making a trip for the first time today, there is a set process we all follow: Input the destination into the phone, study the various routes and then activate the directions. What's more, the pleasant GPS app voice gives step-by step instructions.

I use my GPS even when I'm going to a familiar spot. I drive up to Maine several times each year to visit my mom. The route is very familiar, so there is no risk of getting lost, but I still activate the GPS to make sure there are no traffic issues that would cause me to alter the route. In short, I've come to be totally reliant on my GPS to get me to where I'm going. I'll bet most of us have.

Wouldn't it be nice to have a similar guide in other aspects of our lives? Someone we can turn to have full faith that they will give us good advice and help us to achieve our goals? We're unlikely to find such a guide in our temporal lives, certainly not anything that is as reliable as a GPS is for driving directions. But, as it relates to our spiritual lives, we actually do. We have the Holy Spirit as our guide. Just like our GPS app, when we turn to Him, He will direct us.

Our ultimate destination is Heaven. None of us has been there before, so we don't know the way. Jesus came down to Earth to live among us, show us the way and then open the gates of Heaven for us by His death and resurrection. Despite Jesus teaching us the way, we often get lost in our daily lives, and we don't know how to get there on our own. God knew this would happen, so He sent us the Holy Spirit.

Just like our GPS, we can call on Him at any time, and He will lead us. If we call to Him, if we listen to His guidance, if we trust Him and follow Him, He will lead us to our destination. If there are "traffic" issues along the way, He will help us to navigate through or around them.

If we just say yes, the Holy Spirit will guide us in our daily journeys as well as our life journey. As long as we're following Him, we won't go astray. If we stop following for a time – and all of us will – we can get right back on track by turning to our spiritual GPS.

The process is quite simple and is surprisingly similar to our driving GPS. When we need driving directions, we activate the GPS, trust its guidance, and then follow the guidance. It's the same with the Holy Spirit as our GPS: We activate it (ask Him for help), trust in His guidance and then follow that guidance. Just like it's nice to know that we won't get lost when we're driving, it's very nice to know that we have a way to never get lost in our spiritual life.

Activate. Trust. Follow.

October 6, 2022

IT JUST DOESN'T MAKE SENSE

When I confess my sins and ask for forgiveness, I experience God's love in a unique way. I can personally feel God's mercy and His soothing words...

Growing up, my siblings and I never wanted to incur the anger of my dad. He seldom got mad, but when he did, we were in for it. So you can imagine my fear after throwing a rock through a car window. I was probably four years old, playing in my relative's front yard, down the street from our house. I was pretending to be a baseball player. I didn't have a ball, so I was throwing rocks – not a smart thing to do. The objective was to throw them across the street and onto the field on the other side to my imaginary catcher. I didn't quite make it with one toss, and the rock struck the window of a passing car, shattering it. Who knew a four-year old could throw so hard?

The driver of the car stopped and, understandably, was very upset. My cousin came out to see what the commotion was and went to get my dad. I waited, trembling, sure that I would be grounded for a long, long time. My dad arrived and settled things with the driver. The one-block walk home took an eternity. When we got home, I braced myself for the punishment.

To my amazement, my dad put his arm around me and said, "I know you didn't do it on purpose. It was an accident, but you shouldn't be throwing rocks near the street. Don't do it again." That was it. No punishment! It was unbelievable. I thought for sure I was in big trouble, but my dad understood and had compassion for me. I was so relieved and thankful. And I had learned my lesson.

It's the same with us and our heavenly Father. Throughout our lives, we turn away from God, and He patiently waits for us to return. He has prepared a place in Heaven for each of us, and He desperately wants us to join Him there at the end of our earthly lives. But our sinful nature creates a barrier between us and God and Heaven.

More frequently than I would like to admit, I have had an experience with God similar to the experience with my dad. Typically, it's not a single, traumatic occurrence like the rock and the car, but rather a gradual drifting away. When I realize it, I feel guilty and hesitate to even talk to God because of the guilt. But when I finally turn to God and ask for his mercy, I am amazed at what happens. When I confess my sins and ask for forgiveness, I experience God's love in a unique way. I can personally feel God's mercy and His soothing words, whether spoken through the priest after Confession or directly to me by the Holy Spirit. And I emerge with a skip in my step, just like on that day long ago after the rock-throwing incident.

Our God is so compassionate and loves us so much that He sacrificed His only Son to break the barrier of sin that separates us from Him. Think about it. God gives us everything we need and reserved a place in Heaven for us. How have we responded? We too often take His gifts for granted and gradually drift further away from Him.

What is God's reaction? It should be punishment for our transgressions, just like I thought would be the case with my dad. I thought for sure he would ground me for throwing the rock.

But astonishingly, it's not. God reaches out with compassion. He reminds us that we are already saved by the sacrifice of his Son. When we turn to Him, Jesus puts His arm around us and welcomes us back. Over and over. It just doesn't make any sense! A love so unconditional, so infinite, doesn't make sense. It doesn't have to. But it should make us relieved and thankful. And, hopefully, we've learned our lesson too.

October 26, 2022

A LIGHT IN MY DARKEST HOUR

...because God reached out to me at the time of my greatest need, I am closer to Him now. ... I know one thing for certain: God will never abandon us when we turn to Him.

In 2018 I thought my life was almost perfect. I was doing well in my career at one of the "Big Four" public accounting firms, in my fourth year as the lead partner on the firm's largest audit clients. My wife Jean and I lived in our dream house with panoramic views of Long Island Sound. Our son Paul was off to a good start in his career. We were all healthy and happy. Then, in September, Jean was diagnosed with cancer, and our entire world was turned upside down. She had surgery immediately to remove the cancer and commenced chemotherapy. Jean and I prayed constantly that God would heal her.

Early in 2019, the tests showed the cancer was gone. We were elated. But the feeling was short-lived. A routine ultrasound a few weeks later indicated that the cancer had returned with a vengeance. We, particularly Jean, never lost faith. We continued our prayers, asking God to take away the cancer. However, it was not God's will for Jean to be cured, and she passed away in August 2019.

When praying to Jesus and Mary during the final months of her illness, I was convinced that Jean would be cured. I almost felt Jesus telling me not to worry, so I had complete confidence even as her prognosis worsened. What's more, I have never in my life met a person with stronger faith than Jean, and that faith was never more evident than in those final weeks. So why did God let her die? That's a topic for a separate reflection, but over the past few years, I've become certain that God decided that because of her faith, Jean was ready to move on to eternal life, and that she could accomplish more for Him in Heaven than on earth.

In the days after Jean's death, I lived my life in a complete fog, unable process the fact that she was gone, and that I would never be with her again during my time on earth. And I could not suppress the memories of the moment she died – even though Jean passed very peacefully from this life to the next, the images haunted me.

Exactly one week after Jean passed, I arrived home after having dinner with my in-laws. My son had been with me all week but had gone back to New York earlier in the day. It was my first time alone in the house after her death. As the time approached 10 p.m., the hour that Jean had passed, I became extremely apprehensive. I didn't know how I was going to get through that hour. The feeling continued to get stronger as the clock progressed. My heart was pounding. I didn't want to be alone in the house, but I didn't know where to go. Then, just a few minutes before the top of the hour, I felt the Blessed Mother say to me: "Why don't you go outside on the deck and say a Rosary?"

Jean had a particular devotion to Mary, and we prayed to her often, including the Rosary. We occasionally said our prayers together on the deck; it was private and quiet, with a beautiful view of the Sound. I went out to the deck and did just as Mary suggested. I got lost in my prayer and, when I was done, I realized it was almost 11. That awful hour had passed. I felt at peace. It was the first indication that I was going to get through this – with God's help. It would be tough and take a long time, but during the most difficult days, my thoughts returned to that night, and I was always reassured.

In fact, it was really tough – especially during the first year. But just as Mary spoke to me on that Saturday night, God gently nudged me toward him as the months went by. Sometimes it was a passage in the Bible or a spiritual book that reminded me of His love for me. Another time, when feeling sorry for myself because Jean wasn't here, God quietly told me "Don't worry. She's with Me." Over time, His constant presence pulling me toward Him got me through my grief. While I still miss Jean, I am happy for her because I know she's in Heaven. I also know that she's constantly looking out for me – and all of our loved ones. Moreover, because God reached out to me at the time of my greatest need, I am closer to Him now. I still have a long way to go with my faith, but I know one thing for certain: God will never abandon us when we turn to Him.

August 28, 2021

MY ROAD TO DAMASCUS

"…it became clear to me that God wanted to me spend more time working for Him. At first I didn't know what that meant, but I had an inner peace/trust that He would lead me forward."

Today the Church celebrates the conversion of Saint Paul. His conversion was dramatic and among the most impactful events in the history of the Church. Each of us has been invited by Jesus to make a conversion, albeit for most, it will not be as sudden and transformative as Saint Paul's.

My conversion story commenced in the spring of 2020 after the most challenging year of my life. During 2019 my wife Jean bravely battled a very aggressive form of cancer. She fought to the end, and her faith never wavered. She passed from this life at the end of August. Afterward, I struggled to find my way and a purpose to my life. I returned to work and completely immersed myself to escape the grief I was experiencing. There certainly was plenty to do as we were in the busiest phase of our audit.

We signed off on the audit at the end of February, just before the Covid pandemic hit. I returned home to Connecticut and hunkered down like everyone else. I was still grieving, but with more time on my hands, I started to think about what was next.

My answer came several weeks later while I was watching the mass on television. The churches were closed, so the masses were being said remotely. During the Consecration, I heard a voice say to me "I have other plans for you." It was not a subtle voice. It was loud and clear. It completely surprised me. This had never happened. I looked around the room and saw no one. Gradually, I realized that it was Jesus who had been speaking to me. After the mass, I sat for a long time, trying to make sense of what had just happened. Eventually I went on with my day, but kept flashing back to those words.

Over the next few months it became clear to me that God wanted to me spend more time working for Him. At first I didn't know what that meant, but I had an inner peace/trust that He would lead me forward. After much prayer and reflection, I made the decision to retire from my firm. It was not an easy decision. I had spent my entire career there – almost 35 years – with only four more years before reaching mandatory retirement age. However, I was confident that this was God's will. I kept coming back to those words, "I have other plans for you."

I retired in September, and by then had begun to better discern God's calling. He was asking me to write for Him. I started slowly. Sometimes I still think I'm moving too slowly, but I'm making progress, and it feels great because I believe I'm doing His will. I know it's not me who is doing the writing, but it's the Holy Spirit working through me, and that realization affirms it's God's will.

When Saint Paul experienced his conversion on the road

to Damascus, he was knocked off his horse and blinded. He asked, "Who are you, sir?" Jesus answered, "I am Jesus, of Nazareth whom you are persecuting." Paul's response was incredible: "What shall I do, sir?" (Acts 22:8-10). This was a man who had been relentlessly persecuting the Christians. He thought Jesus was a fraud and sought to wipe out the memory of Him by getting rid of His followers. Then, literally in an instant, he was converted, and spent the rest of his life teaching others about Jesus. What an example for all of us to follow!

Paul was very well educated in the Jewish law and had convinced himself that Jesus didn't fit into the paradigm of those laws. They say old habits die hard. That was not the case for Paul. When Jesus called him, he responded immediately. Granted, the circumstances surrounding his calling were quite dramatic, but still, after a lifetime of being steeped in the Jewish tradition, he converted and never looked back.

Unlike St. Paul, my conversion has been more gradual, perhaps like many of us. However, I feel like I am making progress, and I pray that someday I may experience a complete conversion like his. I've responded to God's call, but as I mentioned, it's been a slow process, – not because I don't want to respond, but because I haven't given myself fully to God as Paul did. I pray that someday I do.

The story of Saint Paul's conversion should act as inspiration and motivation for me and for all of us. Let us strive to listen and act on the words that Ananias spoke to Paul at the end of today's passage: "Now, why delay? Get up and have yourself baptized and your sins washed away, calling upon His name." (Acts 22:16). The time to answer

PAUL E. TUPPER

God's call to move forward with our faith is now.

January 25, 2023

LIVE IN THE MOMENT

He exhorts us to live in the moment. He teaches us to take life one pitch at a time - to trust ourselves and to trust Him in every situation.

Relax! Don't think, just play and have fun! Live in the moment!" It was the climatic point in the game, as the Princeton baseball team trailed by two runs in the ninth inning. My son Paul was at bat. There were two runners on base, two outs and the count on Paul was 0-2. The team was down to its last strike, and everything depended on Paul. This was it. Every parent who has watched their child play a sport has experienced the anxiety of this moment. The outcome of the game will be decided by the play of your son/daughter. I'm pretty sure I was more stressed than Paul was!

Before every game going all the way back to Coach Pitch, I would remind Paul to live in the moment. Don't think about the previous pitch and don't think ahead. Just be in the moment. Too bad I seldom was able to follow my own advice as a spectator at his games! At this pivotal time, never being one to scream to their child in the middle of a game, I did my best to use mental telepathy to communicate the words to Paul.

It may have worked. The pitcher attempted to fool Paul by throwing the same off-speed pitch he had just gotten by him for strike two. This time Paul was ready, and he crushed it for a three-run homer, giving Princeton the lead and ultimately the win. Obviously, Paul's performance had nothing to do with me, but he did, in fact, live in the moment and ultimately experienced a great outcome.

My advice to Paul was in the context of a game, the point being not to overthink the situation, to trust himself and to enjoy each moment as it happens.

Doesn't God want us to do the same thing in our lives? Jesus promises us He will be with us always (Matthew 28:20). He tells us not to worry about anything: "Dismiss all anxiety from your minds" and to let "God's peace, which is beyond all understanding, stand guard over our hearts and minds." (Phil 4:6-7).

Yet, how many of us are actually able to turn off the anxiety signal in our heads? Certainly not me. It seems I'm always worrying about something. You might say that I've perfected the art of worrying. My brain is always going, thinking about the next task on my list and the one after that. And while the nature of the world we live in today gives us plenty of reasons to worry, if we're honest with ourselves, most of what we stress about is quite trivial in the grand scheme of things.

That's precisely what Jesus wants us to avoid. He doesn't want us losing sleep over any matter in our temporal lives and, most especially over things we can't control. The associated stress is not healthy and, moreover, takes our attention away from Him. It's difficult to focus on Jesus while we're worrying about the crisis of the day. Moreover, by definition, worry means that we don't trust God. William Barclay wrote, "Worry about the future is wasted effort, and the future of reality is seldom as bad as the future of our fears." (*The Gospel of Matthew*, Volume One, p. 259; Westminster Press).

Jesus pleads with us not to worry. He wants nothing more than for us to turn our anxieties over to Him and live our lives knowing He is at our side. Barclay further wrote: "Let a man give his best to every situation – he cannot give more – and let him leave the rest to God." (Barclay, p. 260).

I can picture Jesus watching over us like an excited parent. As we're up at the plate – facing both the joys and trials of our lives – He exhorts us to live in the moment. He teaches us to take life one pitch at a time – to trust ourselves and to trust Him in every situation. Jesus implores us not to worry about tomorrow. He preaches "Enough, then, of worrying about tomorrow. Let tomorrow take care of itself." (Matthew 6:34). Trust in Jesus, and live in the moment, every minute of our lives. If we do, we'll hit our share of home runs.

June 6, 2024

PERFECT MOMENTS

He was here, right with me – right within me. Words cannot adequately capture the feeling, which I guess makes sense, as no words can properly describe the love of God...

A partner I once worked for at the Big Four firm often spoke about those perfect moments we all occasionally encounter in our lives. In fact, he wrote a book in which he described such experiences (*Chasing Daylight* by Eugene O'Kelly). In the book, he discussed how these moments often come along unexpectedly and typically last for just a few brief minutes. His message was to be alert and savor them when they occur.

I have tried to follow this advice. I vividly remember the perfect moments in my life to date, like walking along the coast of Maine with my late wife watching the waves crash on the rocks; playing a round of golf with my son at a beautiful course on a warm spring morning; or, sitting on a gorgeous beach with Jessica starring out at the ocean. We've all had them. Perfect moments create a lifetime of happy memories, and we should savor them.

Jesus is the source of all our perfect moments, and we must remember to thank Him each time we experience one. What's more, we can have perfect moments with Jesus as well. Have you ever experienced the sensation of being completely connected to Him? That's a perfect moment. It doesn't happen often for me. When it does it's usually quite brief, but a perfect moment nonetheless. When it does occur, it's an overwhelming experience that usually brings me to tears – tears of joy.

It happened today. I was watching the daily mass on the computer. During the Consecration, I felt that connection to Jesus. Everything else in the world faded away, and He was here, right with me – right within me. Words cannot adequately capture the feeling, which I guess makes sense, as no words can properly describe the love of God, and that's what I experienced. All the challenges of life, all the things that normally distract me during my prayers, all of my fears… They all just melted away during those moments. It humbled me that Jesus would come and be with me.

As I've said many times, it just doesn't make sense. I don't deserve it. I don't give Him the time He deserves, and I'm a sinner. But He comes anyway. In fact, that's precisely why He comes. He comes to each of us. In those brief moments when we're able to block out the distractions and turn to Jesus, He comes and He comforts us. His presence reminds us that He forgives our sins. He wants to be with us, and He wants us to know it. He doesn't want anything in return, except for us to rest in His presence and love Him in return. And that's what brings me to tears. That's our God! He is always there for us when we go to Him, and sometimes He even comes to us.

I wish the moments would last longer. However, even though they're brief, I derive a lot of strength from them. Each one is the ultimate perfect moment. I cherish them.

We all do. And Jesus does too!

    Can you imagine if every moment of our lives could be like this? In fact, that's exactly what we can look forward to. When we pass from this life and enter Heaven, every moment will be a perfect moment. Every minute will be like the perfect moment I had today, only better. Jesus will always be with us for every moment, forever. That's truly perfect.

March 23, 2023

WHAT COULD POSSIBLY BE SO IMPORTANT?

Let's take a few minutes each day to look up, not down. Let's pull our focus away from our phones and look at our surroundings. The presence of God is all around us.

Like most of us, I spend a good portion of the day sitting in front of a computer screen. I try to remind myself to get up and stretch my legs every so often and take in the real world around me. A few minutes ago, I took a break from my work and walked over to the window in my apartment.

When I looked outside, I saw a couple walking their baby in a stroller on the other side of the harbor. It's an absolutely gorgeous day – perfect for a walk. The mother was walking in front pushing the stroller. The father had fallen back several paces. That seemed strange. I wondered why he was so far behind. I looked closer and saw the reason. He had his head buried in his phone, and his fingers were furiously typing away. His wife could have taken a turn, and he would have been completely oblivious. He would have kept right on walking straight ahead. If there had been a cliff in front of him, I think he would have walked right off it.

This guy was totally missing out on a beautiful day and

a perfect moment with his family. What on earth could possibly be so important on that phone? Couldn't he put it down for even a few minutes and experience the real world, live in the moment?

When I was working, I most definitely wasn't a great role model in this regard. My wife and son endured their share of vacations with me spending hours on the phone dealing with client issues. However, certain situations were non-negotiable. When Paul had a baseball game, the phone went into my pocket and didn't come out (unless I was about to take a picture of him in action). Those were perfect moments. When Jean and I did our nightly walks, my phone stayed in my pocket. That was our time together. Those were our perfect moments.

We need to spend quality time with our families, and we need to do that without the distractions of our phones and other devices. We also need that quiet time to be with Jesus. How are we going to see the signs of God if our faces are buried in our phones as we walk?

The vast majority of the people in Jesus' time missed who He was. They were focused on their own lives and their own needs. They were looking down – as if on their phones – and they didn't see God right in front of them.

We may have a tendency to feel indignant toward the people of His time. I know I'm tempted to say, "I wouldn't have missed Jesus. If He were in my town preaching the Good News and healing the sick, I certainly would have realized He was God and followed Him." I wonder if that actually would have been the case.

The young man outside my window certainly didn't see God. Yet the signs were all around him. They were numerous, and they were obvious: the sunny day, the picturesque harbor, his lovely wife and precious child, the gentle fall breeze, the birds singing. All were signs of God and gifts from God. However, he missed them all because there was something on his phone that he deemed more important, and it consumed all his attention.

We all lead busy lives. Most definitely, there are temporal things that require our attention. We can't ignore the demands of our jobs. However, maintaining a sense of balance is important. Let's take a few minutes each day to look up, not down. Let's pull our focus away from our phones and look at our surroundings. The presence of God is all around us. We don't want to be like the people who encountered Jesus when He lived among them. Let's focus our attention on Him. Let's recognize and treasure the perfect moments. What could possibly be more important than experiencing God in our daily lives?

September 10, 2024

JOY

When we're tempted to complain about our trials, we need but reflect on the love God has for us and what's in store for us because of His unfathomable love. We can't help but feel joyful if we focus on that.

Every day, as part of my morning prayers, I read daily spiritual reflections from a few different books. Today there was a singular theme running through them – joy.

In the book *Who Do You Say That I Am* by Cardinal Timothy Dolan, the Cardinal quotes Pope Francis, who said, "…discipleship united for mission will be characterized and effective only with joy." Cardinal Dolan then stated that, "Joy … is a fruit of the Holy Spirit, a gift from God." (*Who Do You Say That I Am*, p. 240; Image).

In *Jesus Always*, Sarah Young wrote that Jesus tells us, "No matter what is happening in your life, you can be joyful in Me because I am your Savior." She then wrote, "This sort of joy is supernatural – powered by the Holy Spirit, who lives in all My followers." (*Jesus Always*, p. 249; Thomas Nelson).

As if to put an exclamation point on this theme, the responsorial psalm for today's mass was "Fill us with your love, O Lord, and will sing for joy!" (Psalm 90).

Clearly, God wants me to better understand and embrace the gift of joy. God wants all of us to embrace the joy that inevitably occurs when we understand – really understand – the depth of His love for us. There is no doubt that His Holy Spirit was at work today, helping me to discern this amazing gift.

Interestingly, both reflections today mention the Holy Spirit: Joy is a "fruit of the Holy Spirit," and it is "powered by the Holy Spirit, who lives in all My followers." It's amazing that Sarah Young used these words. It's as if they are speaking directly to me, given that recently I have been striving to better comprehend how Christ dwells in each of us through His Holy Spirit.

Simply put, if we realize that Jesus truly dwells within us through the Holy Spirit, and that through that Sprit He will guide us through this life and keep us on the path to Heaven, we should be thankful. We should be full of joy! We all can use today's references to joy as a memory jogger when we encounter the many challenges we each face in our daily lives. When we're tempted to complain about our trials, we need but reflect on the love God has for us and what's in store for us because of His unfathomable love. We can't help but feel joyful if we focus on that.

For me, this time of year is particularly challenging as the anniversary of Jean's passing approaches. We each have our own burdens. However, today's reflections helped to ground me and to remind me of why I should be joyful despite my loss. God is with me. He's never going to leave me. And if I acknowledge that His Spirit dwells within me and I allow that Sprit to guide me, I will be on the path to Heaven – the path to true joy, where Jean already resides.

One further personal note regarding joy. The time I spend each day with God brings me joy. I realized that when I'm reading Scripture/spiritual books, praying, writing or just sitting quietly in reflection, I'm in a happy place. I guess that should not be surprising: I'm spending time with God, the source of all of our joy.

So let us allow God to be close to us today by making an effort to be close to Him, even if it's just a few minutes. Let's take time to contemplate and to experience the depth of His love for us, a love so great that He sacrificed His own Son so that we could be with Him for eternity. We never will be able to fully fathom the depth of God's love for us – at least not while we dwell on earth – but even just a partial understanding will bring joy into our lives, no matter what our current circumstances may be. And joy is infectious. Our joy will rub off on those around us, thus bringing Christ into the lives of others.

August 26, 2021

SAYING YES

...there is no more important decision than our response to God's call. ...It lasts for eternity, so we had better get it right.

Mary said, "I am the servant of the Lord. Let it be done to me as you say." (Luke 1:38). This simple response changed the entire course of human history. A young woman – a teenager – was asked to take on a role that was beyond her ability to understand at the time, and yet she was expected to make her decision quickly. The Angel Gabriel had told her that she would conceive out of wedlock and bear a Son who would be the Savior of the world.

Wouldn't most of us want some time to think about it before responding? I know that quite often, when someone springs a request upon me, my instinct is to say no until I've learned more about what will be required of me. Thankfully, for all of us, Mary didn't say no. Remarkably, Mary made her decision quickly, and she never wavered from it thereafter.

Think about the most important decisions you have faced in your life. Certainly, for most of us, one would be marriage. It's a lifetime decision, so it's important we get it right. When I made the decision to ask Jean to marry me so many years ago, it was after months and months of dating.

We talked about marriage frequently. Basically, every day that we spent together, I thought about being married. When I decided to pop the question, I was absolutely certain I wanted to be married to Jean. Fortunately, she agreed and said yes.

Sometimes career decisions are very impactful as well. When asked to take over as the Partner in charge of a very large audit client, I performed a careful analysis before I made my decision. I knew this role would be personally satisfying and would mark the capstone of my career. However, I also knew it would be extremely demanding on my time, thus making it difficult to balance work with my family life. In the end, I accepted the role. In hindsight I was happy with my decision, although at times it was a challenge to achieve a proper work/life balance.

In contrast to our major life decisions, most of us probably don't spend much time on our decision to say yes to God. In fact, in many cases, it's essentially pre-ordained. We are baptized as infants and our parents take us to mass/service when we are children. We grow up in Christian homes where we were taught about God and His Son. We probably just take it for granted that we are Christians, right?

I hope not. While decisions about marriage and our careers are no doubt important, there is no more important decision than our response to God's call. The decision to follow the Lord doesn't expire when we retire from our career or are separated from our spouse in death. It lasts for eternity, so we had better get it right.

Saying yes to God won't impact our lives to the extent Mary's yes impacted hers. However, the decision will require action on our part, and it will affect our lives – in a way that we'll never want to change.

For me, and perhaps many of us, being able to consistently demonstrate my faithfulness to God through my actions is a work-in-progress. I say yes to Jesus with my words as I start every day, but I don't always show it by what I do.

How can we be more resolute and successful with our yes – with our commitment to God? We don't have to look any further than Mary. She lived a faith-based life, and when the calling came through the Angel, she trusted. She trusted God's plan, and she trusted that God would provide her the strength she needed. She submitted herself completely to God. "I am the servant of the Lord. Let it be done to me as you say." (Luke 1:38).

What is our response to God's call?

June 3, 2024

DOING WHAT WE CAN WITH WHAT WE HAVE

...I believe that God not only understands that we might pray while we're commuting or washing the dishes, but that He is smiling when we do so because we found time to be with Him.

Prayer has always been a part of my daily routine. It was ingrained by my parents in my childhood. We said grace every day before dinner. They taught me to pray before I went to sleep at night. They reminded me to offer a prayer when a relative or friend was sick.

The practice of praying continued into my adult life. As a family, we said grace before every meal. Jean and I prayed together before we went to sleep every night. I also prayed at various times during the day when there was some available time. When I was working, my schedule was pretty jammed. On top of the busy days, I typically had a very long commute. So I adapted, saying morning prayers while exercising. The prayers would continue while I was shaving. For several years, I worked at a location in lower Manhattan. I got into the routine of saying the Rosary during the subway ride back and forth (a few decades in the morning and the remaining decades on the way home).

At the time, I never gave much thought to the fact that I was doing other things while praying to God. It seemed better than not praying at all, right? But looking back on it, was this practice really okay? Was I being disrespectful to God? After all, I wasn't giving God the attention He deserved because I was often doing something else while praying.

Then, I remembered the words of St. Paul in his letter to the Thessalonians: "… pray without ceasing" (1 Thessalonians 5:17). According to St. Paul, God wants us to pray always. Furthermore, Jesus encourages us to be persistent in prayer (Luke 18). For most of us, that's hard to do when we have a job that keeps us fully occupied.

So, maybe it was okay that I sneaked in prayers while I was doing other things. I prayed when I could. Jesus certainly understands how busy our daily lives have become. In that regard, I believe that God not only understands that we might pray while we're commuting or washing the dishes, but that He is smiling when we do so because we found time to be with Him. Jesus knows that we're doing what we can with the time we have.

Now that I'm no longer working there is more time to pray, so I don't have to squeeze it in while doing some mundane task. It's possible to have true quiet time with Jesus. That quiet time is important. We need it to be re-energized. We also need it so that we can give thanks to Jesus for all the blessings we have received. Although I had very little spare time when I was working, I wish I knew then what I know now: namely, how important this quiet time is. No matter how busy our lives are, we can always find a few minutes to be alone with our God. It's most definitely something I wish I had done differently.

Fortunately, I don't think God holds it against me. He's a merciful God and, again, I believe He knew I was doing what I could with what I had. The important thing is to do something. We may not be able to pray without ceasing, as St. Paul encourages, but we should take his advice and pray when we can. And, when we pray, we should remember to follow his words in the ensuing passage of his letter: "… pray without ceasing, render constant thanks; such is God's will for you in Christ Jesus." (1 Thessalonians 5:17).

August 7, 2024

BEING DISCIPLES

Any time we perform an act of kindness for someone else, we are disciples of Jesus, even if for a brief moment.

Jesus spent three years on earth teaching His followers to be disciples. What does it mean to be a disciple? I looked up the definition and here is what I found: A disciple is "one who embraces and assists in spreading the teachings of another" (Merriam-Webster).

That is certainly an apt description of the closest followers of Jesus. They listened to His message, embraced it, and spread that message to others. But being a disciple of Jesus goes beyond assisting in spreading His teaching. He expected His disciples to lead by example – to show compassion to others and to bring people to God by helping others: to spread His word by living what He taught. He expects the same of us. How do we respond? How can we be disciples of Jesus?

As I often do, I look to the example set by my late wife, Jean, for guidance. Jean lived an understated life, but she constantly sought ways to help others, and by doing so, brought them closer to God.

Shortly after we were married, Jean had a conversation with my elderly aunt. My aunt mentioned she could no longer drive, and, as a result, she couldn't make it to mass and receive the Eucharist. The next weekend, Jean informed me that we were going to drive down to Aunt Carmela's house, pick her up and take her to church. We quickly settled into a routine each weekend where we would bring Aunt Carmela to mass and afterwards grab dinner together. My aunt was thrilled to get to mass, and I think she liked spending time with us. Looking back, I cherished having that time with my aunt.

Jean listened to my aunt and responded. She brought Aunt Carmela to receive Jesus. By the way, her selfless act also brought Jean and me closer to God and each other. Through her generous actions, Jean embraced the teachings of Jesus. Jean was a disciple of Jesus.

Many years later, Jean learned that another aunt (my mother had eight sisters!) could no longer receive Communion on a regular basis. This time we lived too far away to be able to drive her to church every weekend. But Jean came up with a plan. She contacted Aunt Joan's parish and arranged for someone to bring the Eucharist to her every Sunday. I can still remember receiving a call from the rectory every Sunday morning informing us that the Eucharistic minister was on his/her way to bring Aunt Joan Communion. Aunt Joan was so appreciative of Jean's act of kindness.

Jean enabled Aunt Joan to receive Jesus. Once again, by her thoughtfulness and her actions, Jean embraced the teachings of Jesus. Jean was a disciple of Jesus.

I've given but two examples of how Jean was a disciple of Jesus. The reality is that through her actions, Jean was a disciple of Jesus practically every day of her life.

We tend to think that the actions of the disciples of Jesus

were superhuman and, therefore, we conclude that we can never achieve such status. It's true that many of Jesus' disciples did perform miracles. They made great sacrifices, giving up everything to follow Him. We know that being disciples of Jesus cost many of them their lives. There is no doubt that the first disciples were special people, and they deserve the accolades we give them.

However, as my wife demonstrated in her daily life, we don't have to perform superhuman acts to be disciples of Jesus. There are countless ways that we can embrace and spread His teachings. Any time we perform an act of kindness for someone else, we are disciples of Jesus, even if for a brief moment.

What made Jean different from most is that she innately thought of others first – before she thought of herself. The disciples undoubtedly did the same thing. She and they were following the example set by Jesus with His own life. We can be disciples too if we follow their lead.

September 28, 2023

PAYING IT FORWARD

It didn't take long for the early followers to emulate the Apostles, thereby cascading the positive momentum. Soon, the early followers were being called Christians (of Christ). That must have made the Apostles really proud.

When I walked into his office and he introduced himself, all my pre-conceived notions vanished. I was a young manager at my public accounting firm. I had spent my seven-year career up to that point at one of the firm's satellite offices. One day a position opened as the lead manager of one of the larger financial services clients, and I was assigned to the job. The client was based in New York City, which meant that I would be transferring there.

The New York office had a certain reputation – it seemed like Type A personalities abounded! I had experienced some of it first-hand in firm-wide meetings and on calls. My personality was different – reserved and laid back. How was I going to fit into this culture?

Meeting the partner for the first time was a nerve-wracking experience. He was the lead partner serving a very important client, and he had spent his entire career in the New York office. I prepared for the worst. Would he grill me with questions from the start? If I said something he didn't like, would he throw me out of his office? Who knew?

It only took a second for me to find out. He looked at me with a warm smile and welcomed me to the New York office. We spent a long time talking about everything, everything that is but work. This guy most definitely did not fit my self-crafted image of a New York office member (Eventually I would find out that almost no one did!). I in time realized that in addition to being a really nice person, he was an exceptional partner.

The more I worked with him, the more I liked what I saw. I carefully observed how he went about his job and tried to emulate his many positive traits. Over time, I made small tweaks to my style. It's fair to say that he had a significant influence on the type of professional I became.

Years later, several colleagues observed that our styles were similar, which I viewed as a compliment. Moreover, a few of my direct reports over the years asked me to mentor them, which made me feel like I was paying it forward. The senior partner had positively influenced me, which in turn cascaded down to those whom I worked with.

By analogy, Jesus was that senior partner for His Apostles. There was something about Jesus that attracted the Apostles to Him from the start. They wanted to know more about Him. And the more time they spent with Jesus, the more they learned and the more they tried to emulate Him. They were never going to be Jesus, but they could and did become leaders in their own right. They put a priority on their relationship with Jesus, and they benefited by better understanding Him and eventually became more like Him.

After Jesus ascended to Heaven, the Apostles struck out on their own. They put into practice what they had learned from Jesus and started to build the Church. It didn't take long for the early followers to emulate the Apostles, thereby cascading the positive momentum. Soon, the early followers were being called Christians (of Christ). That must have made the Apostles really proud. The Apostles had paid it forward.

Just like the Apostles, we are students of Jesus. He teaches us through His Word, which we absorb every time we read the Gospels. He brings people into our lives who, by their words and actions, demonstrate what it is to be a Christian, a follower of Christ. They inspire us to emulate them and become better Christians.

Moreover, Jesus dwells within us through His Spirit, and that Spirit guides us each day, helping us to spread His Love to those we encounter. As we spend more time with Jesus, we want to emulate Him – become more like Him. And when we become more like Him, we, in turn, pay it forward.

August 14, 2024

OUR REASSURANCE

...Jesus is there for us when we need reassurance. He knows when we need it. After all, He's God. He is waiting for us to ask and He will respond...

"Take your finger and examine my hands. Put your hand in my side. Do not persist in your unbelief but believe!" (John 20:27). Can you imagine what Thomas was thinking when Jesus spoke these words to him? One week earlier, Thomas had been skeptical as the Apostles recounted their experience with Jesus, and he made a very strong statement. We all know the words. They gave Thomas the nickname "Doubting Thomas."

When the Risen Lord appeared a week later and spoke directly to Thomas, His response probably seemed harsh to the skeptic and the other Apostles in the room. If I were Thomas, I might have just put my head down and mumbled an apology to Jesus. Instead, Thomas didn't sulk at all. He said something extraordinary in response: "My Lord and my God." (John 20:28). With his brief declaration, Thomas was the first Apostle to publicly acknowledge Jesus as God.

The faith of Thomas was on full display when He saw Jesus, quite a contrast from the "Doubting Thomas" just a week earlier. Sure, it certainly helped that he saw Jesus in the flesh. But none of the other Apostles had proclaimed Jesus was God one week earlier, nor on that second Sunday.

Thomas' faith isn't consistent with a doubter.

There may another explanation for Thomas' reaction to the Apostles after they saw Jesus. Maybe it wasn't so much doubt that Thomas was feeling as much as it was his need for reassurance. The Apostles were suffering because their teacher had been killed. They had traveled with Him for three years, saw Him perform miracles, were taught by Him, were close to Him. And suddenly He was gone. I'm sure they were in a state of shock.

Then some women claimed to have seen Him alive. John and Peter had gone to the tomb to find it empty. They were hopeful, but they needed reassurance. Jesus gave that reassurance to them when He appeared in the upper room on the first day of the week. The impossible had happened. Jesus had risen from the dead.

Thomas needed that same reassurance. And Jesus knew it. Jesus came back to the room a week later, knowing Thomas would be with the others. He came for Thomas. He reassured Thomas, and that reassurance emboldened Thomas. The faith Thomas had in his heart came to the surface as he acknowledged Jesus as "my Lord and my God." By the way, I don't think Jesus was scolding Thomas with the words He spoke. I think Jesus was excited to be able to reassure Thomas (notice the exclamation point in the Gospel passage).

In the same way, Jesus is there for us when we need reassurance. He knows when we need it. After all, He's God. He is waiting for us to ask and He will respond, just as He did when Thomas asked.

My wife and I needed reassurance in a big way during her pregnancy. We were expecting our first child – a time that should be filled with happiness and joyful anticipation. However, we were worried, very worried. An ultra-sound had identified a major concern with our baby. We prayed and prayed but we still worried. The doctor had performed several procedures to address the issue; however, the procedures were unsuccessful. We continued to pray, but our worries remained.

One day we were on our way to the hospital for yet another procedure. During the ride we continued to pray. As I drove, I looked in the rearview mirror. I saw the image of the Blessed Mother sitting in the back seat with the most determined look on her face. That image told me that she wasn't going to let anything bad happen to our baby. That was our reassurance, God telling us not to continue worrying but to believe.

When we got to the hospital, the doctor went through his usual routine and performed an ultrasound prior to the procedure. After a few minutes, he turned to us with a puzzled look on his face. He informed us that the problem had disappeared. There was no need for another procedure. The doctor couldn't explain what had happened. But we could. Anything is possible with God.

Life brings challenges. We face them as best we can, but sometimes the challenges seem overwhelming. We may feel alone, struggling to maintain a sense of hope. In those circumstances, we need reassurance, just like Thomas did and just like my wife and I did. Jesus is waiting. He knows when we need reassurance, and He will provide it. And when He does, He will excitedly exclaim, "Do not persist in your unbelief, but believe!"

April 19, 2024

IT'S A TEAM EFFORT

...we are not alone in our journey. We have lots of people to help us. In fact, we each are part of a team - a spiritual team.

Tonight is the NCAA men's college basketball championship game. It's one of my favorite sporting events of the year. The energy will be palpable, even for those of us watching on television. It's what each of the 150-plus teams has been striving for since the season began five months ago, and now there are only two teams left. They've practiced together every day to achieve their goal of playing for the championship. They pull for each other. They work together unselfishly for the greater good – in this case, winning the game. They console each other during tough times. They prevail together. They achieve their goal together. They win as a team.

All of us have been a part of a team at one time or another. Perhaps we were on a sports team when we were young. Maybe we worked as part of a team performing a volunteer service. Regardless, we all have experienced the success we can achieve when working as a team. Furthermore, I'm sure we can remember how exhilarating it feels when the moment comes as we hit our stride and everything just clicks.

During my career as an accountant, I never worked

alone. I was always part of a team. Our goal was to complete the audit of our client's financial statements. It was not a job for one person. We all had our roles. In the early days, I was the junior guy, and often my responsibilities were to make copies and get coffee for the more senior people. Pretty menial tasks, but I did them because it was my role on the team. As my skills developed, I spent more time with client personnel, working through various accounting issues. In my later years, I was fortunate to lead my audit teams. It brought me tremendous satisfaction to help mentor the younger team members and witness their development over the course of the audit. And no, I did not ask them to get me coffee!

I definitely miss the euphoria we experienced in late February each year when we signed off on the audit after months and months of hard work and long hours (often very long hours). We succeeded as a team.

Just like we have goals for work, we have goals in our spiritual lives. We want to develop a closer relationship with Jesus and strive to be better Christians. Our ultimate goal – our definition of winning -- is to make it to Heaven when we pass from this life.

Fortunately for us, we are not alone in our journey. We have lots of people to help us. In fact, we each are part of a team – a spiritual team. I have a top-notch spiritual team, which is good because I definitely need a lot of help. My team includes my significant other, family members, the parish pastor, the deacon in my parish and several of my close friends. We all have the same goals, and we all support each other during our journey.

And if that isn't enough, we have literally an army of

supporters who want nothing more than for us to join them in Heaven. Just to name a few, we have the loved ones who have gone before us: parents, spouses, grandparents, aunts and uncles. We have our guardian angel who is constantly looking out for us. We have our patron saint and, in fact, all of the saints. Then, we have the big guns: Saint Joseph and the Blessed Mother. Any time we're feeling that our daily struggle is wearing us down, we need only think of all of the supporters we have – some pushing, others pulling us toward Heaven.

Finally, most importantly, we have our team leader – Jesus. He is with us every step of the way. We hear often that the best leaders are the ones who lead by example. Well, Jesus certainly did that. We couldn't have a better team leader and one who is so vested in us achieving our success. As long as we're committed to being part of His team, there's no way we can lose. With Jesus, winning is guaranteed.

April 3, 2023

LESS IS MORE

...when we remember to slow down and spend quiet time with God, we will have an opportunity to consider what's most important in our lives.

I recently read a newspaper article suggesting that people are more successful when they are asked to do less rather than more. Addition by subtraction. The author referenced a research study that demonstrated that, contrary to conventional wisdom, the most successful performers often didn't take on more and more tasks to get ahead. Those who had less tasks to do were able to perform them better. Furthermore, they had more time to think strategically about the assignment and, thus, often figured out a way to do the task better. I have often used the phrase "less is more." That was the premise of the article.

Boy, do I wish this research study had existed 34 years ago when I was starting my career. It might have saved me a lot of stress and freed up more hours for sleep! Joking aside, I've long been a proponent of less is more and tried to apply it. For example, in preparing a presentation for my client's Board of Directors, I gradually realized that one or two pages of key messages are usually much more effective than twenty pages filled with data. Similarly, when giving guidance to a co-worker, I came to realize that it's often better to provide conceptual advice rather than prescriptive directions. Such advice usually enables the individual to get to the right place on his/her own, which helps their development.

As those who know me will attest, I tend to overthink most aspects of my life, including my faith. In particular, as it relates to my spiritual life, I often think that I'm not doing enough. That very well may be true. It's also true that I use this line of thinking to drive myself to work harder in just about everything I do. That's probably not a bad thing. However, the conclusions from the research study are a good reminder about being focused.

Just like with one's career, perhaps doing less may help me to get more accomplished. First, those items that I deem important are likely to be done better, as I will have more time to focus on them. Secondly, I will have more time to listen to God and to reflect – to think strategically about my faith and what God is calling me to do.

There's certainly precedent for this in the Gospels. Jesus most definitely had a critical mission to carry out. He had a limited amount of time on earth in which to teach His disciples and start His church. Yet, there are numerous instances where He seeks downtime. The Gospel writers tell us of how Jesus goes off by Himself to pray, usually before or after a big event occurs. We also read how Jesus instructs His disciples to take some time and rest after they had come back from their journeys spreading his Word (MK6:31). For Jesus, less was more. He periodically needed time to reassess, to think about how best to accomplish His mission. And most importantly, He needed time alone with His Father, for guidance and for encouragement.

It can and should be the same for me and for all of us.

Stopping to take time out of our busy day to be with God is not wasted time. On the contrary, it is valuable time, and it will provide multiple benefits. It will reaffirm that we're carrying out the plan God has set forth for us. Or if we're not, it will help us to recalibrate. It also will help us to deepen our relationship with Jesus and, therefore, increase our faith. Just like any relationship, the more time we spend on it, the stronger it will become.

The research study concluded that when people are not overwhelmed with many tasks, they have time to think about the ones they are doing and perform them better. Similarly, when we remember to slow down and spend quiet time with God, we will have an opportunity to consider what's most important in our lives. Connecting with God will also help us to ensure we are focusing what He desires and that we perform those tasks well. Less is more.

June 07, 2022

GOD'S SCHEDULE

If we let Him work on His time and not ours, we will be able to enjoy the many gifts He bestows on us, just as Abraham did. ... if we let God manage our schedules, He will get us to our ultimate destination.

I like to attend daily mass. The church typically is not full, so there are less distractions. That helps me to better focus on why I'm there in the first place. Receiving the Eucharist is a great way to start the day. Furthermore, although the homilies are usually very short, oftentimes I find little nuggets in the priest's words that resonate. Less is more!

I found one of those nuggets recently. The priest made a simple but very insightful comment: "God doesn't work on our schedule." His comment was in the context of the reading from the Old Testament in which God tells Abraham he and Sarah will have a son despite their advanced age. In this story, the message is that Abraham was patient and God blessed him. Similarly, we need to be patient and wait for the gifts that God lavishes on us. For someone who likes to have everything run according to his well-scripted schedule, these are hard words for me to take in.

As I reflected on these words, I realized that just the day before I got myself all worked up over my schedule. I needed to drive my car from Connecticut into New York City to drop it off for my son, so he could use it for a trip with his friends. Being that it was just before a holiday weekend, I expected the traffic to be heavy. Accordingly, I fixed a timeline in my head to stay ahead of the traffic.

Prior to my departure, I became increasingly apprehensive about the potential congestion. I departed at my designated time but wasn't on the highway for more than a mile when the traffic came to a dead stop. I looked ahead, and I saw the dreaded orange sign on the side of the road: construction, one lane closed. My anxiety turned to anger as I sat in the traffic for what seemed like an hour. I kept looking at my GPS and watching the arrival time slip further back. When I had finally cleared the construction, I wasn't able to calm down for quite a while.

Looking back on that experience with the benefit of hindsight, I realize how silly I had been. I had nowhere to be on that particular day, so why did I have a schedule? What's more, even if I did have somewhere else to be, there was absolutely nothing I could do once I was mired in the construction delay. But yet, I had set my schedule and I got all off-kilter when it was put at risk.

Unfortunately, it happens often with me. I set a plan and I feel like I have to achieve it. As people often say, "Man plans and God laughs." God wants us to entrust our lives to Him. He's not going to take care of everything – certainly I can't expect Him to clear the road for me to make a meaningless deadline – but He can guide our lives and our actions. If we let Him work on His time and not ours, we will be able to enjoy the many gifts He bestows on us, just as Abraham did. Finally, if we let God manage our schedules, He will get us to our ultimate destination.

There is another lesson in my travel story. I'm always looking to find quiet time to be with God. Looking back, I missed a terrific opportunity while stuck in traffic. There was no one else in the car and I had plenty of time on my hands with nothing to do. Instead of grousing over the delay, I could have talked to God or just quietly meditated. It would have been time very well spent, and it would have improved my mood too. When things aren't going our way, turning to God will always make things better.

One footnote on my travel story: The ultimate irony is that I actually arrived within 5 minutes of the original time I had set in my head. As my better half will tell me, that's on time!

July 5, 2023

OVERWHELMED BY PEACE

Jesus wants me ⁻ He wants all of us ⁻ to let His peace take over our minds and hearts. He wants His peace to be so powerful that we don't ⁻ we can't ⁻ focus on anything else. In other words, let it overwhelm us!

"Come into my presence. Feel my peace. Let my peace overwhelm you."

I occasionally go through phases where the sheer number of tasks I face seems overwhelming. We all do. It happened more frequently when I was working. There would be stretches where my to-do list at work seemed to be constantly expanding. On top of that, I would stress about balancing my time at work with the chores to be done at home, while making sure that I wasn't neglecting my family. It all seemed overwhelming, and I longed for everything to slow down. We've all been there. Even though I've been retired for a few years, occasionally I still get the feeling.

"Come into my presence. Feel my peace. Let my peace overwhelm you." These were the words Jesus spoke to me today during my quiet time with Him. For several days, I had been stressing about all the things going on in my life. In a word, I had allowed myself to become overwhelmed.

As a result, I had not been successful in blocking out the noise and allowing Jesus to be present with me, even for a few moments.

Today started out no differently. I tried to relax and clear my mind to be with Jesus. But immediately I started thinking about all the items on my list -- what had to get done before the day ended. I was about to give up, thinking there was no use trying to quietly meditate with Jesus. I just wasn't going to be able to put myself in His presence.

Just at that point, I had the experience of being pulled into a very serene place. Everything became calm, and I could feel His presence. And, I thought, "Peace." It was right then that I heard Jesus' words "Come into my presence. Feel my peace. Let my peace overwhelm you." The last line really resonated with me – "let my peace overwhelm you." An interesting choice of words by Jesus – overwhelm. I had always associated that word with stress, as I'm sure most of us do. How often do we say, "I'm overwhelmed at work?" It's not a coincidence that I was feeling overwhelmed in this way when Jesus spoke to me. His choice of the word was not random. Nothing Jesus does is random.

The experience made me reflect on the scene in John's Gospel when Jesus appears to the disciples after He had risen. They were all in one room and had locked the doors out of fear of the Jews. They were afraid – perhaps overwhelmed. He came and stood before them and said, "Peace be with you," (John 20:19), not once but twice. The fear that had consumed the disciples turned into joy once they were in the presence of Jesus. What's more, that peace strengthened them to leave the room where they had been hiding and begin to proclaim the Good News. In sum, they were overwhelmed by His peace. It fundamentally changed them.

Jesus wants me – He wants all of us – to let His peace take over our minds and hearts. He wants His peace to be so powerful that we don't – we can't – focus on anything else. In other words, let it overwhelm us! Powerful peace: it may sound like an oxymoron but, wow, how amazing it can be. If we let the peace of Christ take control of our lives, it will fundamentally change us. And, if we all embrace His peace, it might just change the world. Let His peace overwhelm you.

April 26, 2022

BE ALERT

He extends an invitation to us every day. We just need to be alert and respond to His presence in our lives.

It's important to be focused on what we're doing. When we're driving in the car, we need to be alert. When I'm paying my bills, it's important that I'm alert – I certainly don't want to accidentally overpay! We all hope that our doctor is alert when he/she is performing an important procedure.

What happens when we're alert? We become aware of the more subtle developments that are easy to miss. When I'm driving, I'll probably see the car right in front of me even if my mind is wandering at that moment. However, unless I'm really paying attention, I may not notice the car that's about to pull out of the parking lot and veer into my lane. Being alert means being cognizant of all of one's surroundings and being able to react and respond accordingly.

It's the same with our relationship with Jesus. When we're complacent, we are more likely to drift, which can endanger our relationship with Him. When we're focused on Him, we will become much more aware of His presence in our everyday lives.

A few years ago I spent a few weeks on Long Island with

my son. He had found a nice rental in a quiet neighborhood called Springs and suggested that we get away for a bit. He was working remotely during the day, so I had plenty of time for reading and relaxing. My favorite part of the day was an afternoon walk. It was mid-May and the weather was perfect – warm enough to walk without a coat but not too hot. I took the same route each day, which led me to a marina about a mile away. The setting was beautiful. In addition to the great weather, the flowers were in full bloom, the lawns had become a plush green, the birds were out in force singing and lots of boats were moored in the water. The experience was incredible. It was easy to see God's hand in these beautiful scenes.

During the walk I would talk (silently!) to Jesus. It was a special time. There was no one around, and therefore there were no distractions. I was focused. I actually felt like I was conversing with Jesus. I would talk to Him about whatever was on my mind. Occasionally, a thought would pop into my head, and I realized it was Jesus responding. Sometimes I wouldn't hear anything in response, but I felt a sense of peace. Other times, I would find a solution to a problem I had been discussing with Him. But there were several constants: Each time I was focused on being with Jesus, and each time I would finish the walk refreshed and happy. I reflect on those weeks frequently, especially the walks, and it always brings a smile to my face. I call it "going back to my Springs."

During one of my last walks prior to departing, I was talking to Jesus about His plans for me. I was speculating about various possibilities. In response, Jesus didn't say, "I want you to do this or do that." Instead, what I heard was "Be alert." I immediately started to focus on my surroundings – the trees, the birds, the boats on the water – thinking that I would notice something. I soon understood, however, I wasn't going to see something right then, and it wasn't going to be obvious. Jesus told me to be alert precisely because whatever signs He was planning to give me were going to be subtle, not obvious.

As I look back on it, there is no doubt that I was alert during those walks. I was focused only on Jesus, and consequently, I really connected with Him for that hour each day. I picked up on His responses to my thoughts. I was more aware of His presence in everything around me. I was "locked in" during those walks.

Unfortunately, my focus didn't take lasting root. When I returned home, life's daily distractions intervened. I got out of my regular rhythm with Jesus. To be sure, there are occasions when I feel like I did on those daily walks, but they don't occur regularly because I'm not properly focused. Frequently I remind myself to "go back to my Springs."

Jesus was very intentional in waiting until the end of the trip to admonish me to be alert. He knew it was going to be more difficult to stay focused when I got back home. I'm pretty sure He cherished those moments together as much as I did, and He wanted them to continue. He wants to have those moments with all of us. He extends an invitation to us every day. We just need to be alert and respond to His presence in our lives.

March 16, 2023

I'VE GOT THIS

…It's important to turn to God in times of stress. And in this case when I finally did, the most remarkable thing happened. My Father in Heaven said to me: "I've got this. Don't worry about it."

We all can think of times in our lives when we needed our fathers. When I struggled on a big test at school or when someone made fun of me on the playground, I went to my dad for support. His response was always comforting, and I would stop worrying. When I was really young, I couldn't wait for my dad to get home from work. I would sit down next to him on the couch and tell him about my day.

I've had similar experiences with my son, Paul. He's now 27, but we shared many moments as he was growing up, whether it was after a tough baseball game or a challenging day at school. We still do, as we'll often talk when he's had a difficult day at work. And as his father, I constantly worry about him, even more so in the years since his mom passed away.

Recently I've been particularly anxious about Paul's trip to Europe; he departs later today. He will soon start a new job and is taking some time off beforehand. He works in the finance industry, so his career involves long hours and quite a bit of stress. He needs this break before he jumps into what will likely be an even more demanding job. He and some friends will be traveling to Greece and Croatia.

I'm thrilled for him, but I'm nervous. I always worry when he travels by plane, but this will be his first trip to Europe without me going with him, and that's making me more nervous than usual. On top of that, the Covid pandemic, which had seemed to be in the rearview mirror, has again flared up. Since he will be with large groups of people, the risk of contracting Covid is higher, adding to my anxiety.

Despite knowing that God hears and answers our prayers, I have not been able to shake my feeling of nervousness about Paul's trip. I keep thinking of all the things that could go wrong. I'll pray to Jesus about it and feel better for a bit. Then I get nervous again.

While I was saying yet another prayer, I thought about God being our Father – our Dad. The Holy Spirit then reminded me of a text Paul sent me just yesterday: "Thanks dad! I can take the lashing later but kinda need my dad right now!!"

Paul had some cosmetic dental work done two days ago – before his big Europe trip. I didn't think the timing was a good idea, being just before a long international trip, and told him so on numerous occasions prior to the procedure. Despite my advice, Paul went ahead with it. He told me that the dentist had assured him that the procedure was very simple, and there would be no pain or problems afterward.

Well, despite those assurances, Paul experienced some complications yesterday. In his text, he was thanking me for telling him that I would pray for a safe trip, but also asking me to ease up on the "I told you so" lecture. He needed my compassion and support. His text brought tears to my eyes, and I realized that sometimes I have to remember to still be a dad.

And then I suddenly realized that's also what I need right now. I kinda need my Dad. I need to turn this over to my heavenly Father, to trust in Him to keep Paul safe (and without any further complications from the dental work!).

Just like Paul turns to me when he needs help, and just like I turned to my dad when I needed reassurance, I realized that it's important to turn to God in times of stress. And in this case when I finally did, the most remarkable thing happened. My Father in Heaven said to me: "I've got this. Don't worry about it. He's going to have a good time." And with that, my anxiety went away. I stopped worrying. It was like a switch flipped in my mind.

In the gospels, Jesus encourages us to have childlike faith, where we place complete trust in Him. I think He was gently reminding me of that with my reaction to Paul's trip. When we're facing a challenge or are worried about something, we can turn it over to our Father with total trust, and He will say, "I've got this."

September 4, 2021

WORKING FOR GOD

...we will always get a great return on our investment of time with God. It's absolute ⁃ the only sure bet we have in life.

On my morning walk in my lower Manhattan neighborhood today, I watched the crowd of commuters get off the ferry and head to their jobs. I observed the workers on a delivery truck unload daily supplies for the local restaurant. I watched the construction workers start their day at the giant office building near my apartment. It was a beautiful morning, and the world was waking up and going to work. As I observed all of this, I thought about my working days, some 34 years' worth, many right at that same office building. God blessed me with a successful career, and I enjoyed my time with my co-workers. But if I'm being honest, I don't miss the job. In fact, I thank God every day for nudging me to retire.

Then it occurred to me. I'm still working – only I work for God now. He's my boss. He's our boss. At our jobs, our supervisors will hand out assignments and give instructions. With my new boss, I need to make sure that, at the start of every day, I take time to listen for instructions. Often there may not be specific guidance. My to-do list isn't always filling the page. But I think that's intentional. I believe that God wants us to spend quality time with Him.

Furthermore, He knows it will be a process to transition us to our next career working for Him.

Even now, when it doesn't seem like I'm doing much, I actually am. I believe that I'm in training for the plan God has for me. Through the direction of the Holy Spirit, I've been spending more time reading, praying, writing and listening (although I never do enough of the latter). At the start of every day as I get out of bed, I say "Jesus, help me to perform at a high level for you today." When I was working at the public accounting firm, I would remind myself each morning to perform at a high level that day. But now it really counts – I'm working for God.

With whatever our endeavors are, we want to maximize their value. With our job, we want to excel and thus be viewed positively by our supervisors. If we're making investments with our resources, we want to maximize the returns.

I spent my career doing audits of large financial institutions. One of the metrics my clients closely monitored was return on investment, or ROI. The higher the ROI, the more profit an investment would generate for the institution. Of course, there was always the possibility of a negative ROI, which was not good.

On the contrary, we will always get a great return on our investment of time with God. It's absolute – the only sure bet we have in life. Furthermore, it's a virtuous circle. We obtain a positive return on our investment with God. And in turn, by spending time with Him, we can give God a return on His investment in us – His love. God's love was manifested in the sacrifice of His Son and also is present every day through His Son dwelling in us. As it is with everything that comes from God, He gives us so much more than we can ever give Him.

If we truly grasp the unfathomable goodness of God we should want to make Him happy, so giving of ourselves to Him should be something that we want to do every day. We should want to excel in our work for God because He's our boss. We should want to invest in our relationship with Him. It's an investment that's a sure bet. It will give us a ROI of infinity – eternal life.

August 5, 2021

OUR FATHER IS PROUD

...if we're seeking to do His will, if that's constantly on our minds, we will have a much better chance of succeeding. And that fact alone will make our heavenly Father proud of us.

"You are my beloved Son. On you, my favor rests." (Mark 1:11). The Father spoke these words to Jesus after He was baptized. With them, God made it clear who Jesus was to everyone listening. However, the Father's words also were meant for Jesus Himself. Yes, Jesus was God, but He also was human, and like us, I think He drew strength from the fact that His Father was proud of Him.

We see other instances in the Gospels where the Father builds up Jesus. Shortly after Jesus entered Jerusalem to ultimately face His death, the Father spoke to Him again. As Jesus foretold of His Passion to an audience of Greek visitors, a voice from the sky proclaimed: "I have glorified it [Jesus' name] and will glorify it again." (John 12:28).

God's words assured Jesus that He supported Him, that Jesus was doing His will, that He was proud of Him.

When we were kids, weren't we ecstatic when our parents showed pride in us? When we did well on a test in school, didn't we rush home to tell our parents the good news? And perhaps hope for a special treat in response?!

We needed that assurance. It's no different now that we're adults. We get that necessary boost from our spouses, sometimes still from our parents and sometimes even from our children.

When I received a good report card in school, I couldn't wait to show my parents. Each time they told me that they were proud of me. That meant so much to me, especially when it came from my dad – he didn't hand out the compliments freely, but he made sure I knew he was proud when I did well in school. That didn't change as I got older. Every time I got a promotion at work or was assigned to a prestigious client, I called my dad to tell him the good news. I wanted him to share my joy, but equally, it made me feel good to know he was proud. It drove me to work hard and strive for continued success.

It's part of our human condition to want those closest to us to be proud of us. In His humanity, Jesus needed it, too. And, like Jesus, we also draw strength for our spiritual journey by knowing our heavenly Father is proud of us.

Yes, we draw strength when we are confident that God is proud of us. However, how often do we proactively seek to make God proud by our actions? As kids, we always wanted to make our parents proud. Do we take deliberate steps to make God proud or do we just hope it will happen?

Jesus lived every day seeking to do the will of His Father. God knows we're human, so He doesn't expect us to accomplish His will 100 percent of the time. However, if we're seeking to do His will, if that's constantly on our minds, we will have a much better chance of succeeding. And that fact alone will make our heavenly Father proud of us.

April 22, 2024

OUR INNER CIRCLE

We merely need to remind ourselves that Jesus is part of our inner circle. He's one of the precious few we can turn to in all circumstances.

Last night I received some really good news. Over the previous several weeks, I had been struggling to find someone to edit my writing. I believe that I'm ready to publish my first book, but I've been stuck. I couldn't find an editor and, not having a background in writing, I didn't know how to go about looking for one.

Fortunately, a close friend, a writer whose work regularly appears in numerous religious publications, put me in touch with a colleague who is an editor. He called me last night to inform me that he had agreed to edit my reflections.

I was ecstatic! I couldn't wait to share my great news, and so the first thing I did was to call Jessica. When she answered, I don't think I even said hello; I just blurted out, "I have some good news. I have an editor!" Jess almost came through the phone. She was happy for me and was as excited as I was. The news was indeed great, but it was made all the better by having someone to share it with. It's such a blessing to have that special person in your life to share your joy.

It works the same way with difficult situations. When

we receive a worrisome health diagnosis or when we face a career-threatening issue at work, we go to that one person who we know understands what we're feeling and will stick with us throughout any situation. I certainly have leaned on Jess many times. I also no doubt needed the support of those closest to me when Jean passed. We all need the support of those in our inner circle.

Have we made Jesus part of our inner circle? He promised to be with us always. In his last discourse to the Apostles, He told them "I will not leave you orphaned. I will come back to you." (John 14:18). Jesus kept His promise. He came back to the Apostles a few weeks later through the Holy Spirit. He came to us too. He dwells within us through the Holy Spirit. He is with us – within us – every second of our lives to share our highs and our lows.

After I hung up with the editor, my first instinct was to call Jess. A little while after she and I spoke, it dawned on me that God was responsible for what had happened, so I said a prayer of thanks to Him. But why wasn't that my first instinct? After all, God is responsible for everything that had occurred up to now. He blessed me with the calling to write for Him. His Spirit has been working within me to inspire the words I write. And when I needed help moving forward, He showed me the way. Everything that I've been doing with my writing is for God and because of God. If ever there was a time to turn to Jesus first to share my joy, this was it.

I'm quite certain that, if I had received bad news or was facing a challenging situation, I would have turned to God immediately and asked for help. Why wasn't that my initial reaction when I received good news?

Fortunately, it doesn't require a major effort to fix this situation. We merely need to remind ourselves that Jesus is part of our inner circle. He's one of the precious few we can turn to in all circumstances. I start each day with either a phone call or a text message to Jessica. I'm sure almost all of us do the same with our loved one. We can do the same thing with Jesus. We can start each day with a prayer to Him. It only takes a few seconds.

Before we even get out of bed, we can thank Jesus for the blessings we will receive throughout the day. We can thank Him in advance for being with us every step of the way. We can ask Jesus for help during the challenging situations we will encounter. Finally, most simply but most importantly, we can thank Jesus for his love for us and tell Him we love Him. Jesus, thank you for being part of my inner circle.

August 12, 2024

IN OUR WEAKNESS

If we would only ask, Jesus will help us to let Him lead our lives. If we allow ourselves to be humble and weak, we will become strong because Jesus will occupy a more prominent place in our life.

When we are weak, He is strong." It's such a powerful and reassuring statement regarding Jesus. I heard it proclaimed at mass today and took some time to meditate on the words. I realized that this statement is applicable on several levels. First, we are, as human beings, weak because of our sin. We can't save ourselves, but Christ can and He did. He had the strength to face the cross and death, and that strength overcame our weakness.

Secondly, when we are struggling with something or are down in the dumps, we can turn to Jesus, and He becomes our strength. If we just let Him, He provides the strength we need to overcome the most difficult situations. I certainly know from my own experience. When I was at my lowest point – dealing with the unimaginable loss of my wife – Jesus and His Mother were there for me. They got me through an extremely tough period and gently nudged me toward them. I found strength that I never knew I had. It came from Jesus.

Thirdly, Jesus asks us to become weak in terms of our

egos and standing in the temporal world and try to put Him and the needs of others before our own. This is the most difficult of the three dimensions. The first dimension – overcoming sin -- was done by Jesus for us. We didn't do anything. For the second, we just need to turn to Jesus and ask for help, and He will provide. For the third, however, we must make the conscious decision to step back and put Jesus and others before ourselves – not just one time but every day of our lives. It requires action on our part.

We've all met people who are able to put others before themselves. I can think of a former boss who, no matter what he was dealing with professionally, always was thinking of others. He was the lead partner on one of our largest and most challenging clients, so he was constantly dealing with multiple issues. Once, while he was struggling with a particularly difficult client matter, he called me into his office. He knew I was fretting about my own issues – which were trivial in comparison to his. He pulled out a gift box and gave it to me, saying, "I thought this might cheer you up." It was a tie with the insignia of my alma mater on the front. I was touched by his empathy, and that he thought of me during a difficult time for him. That's what Christ did and what He wants us to do for others and for Him. In our weakness…

My late wife constantly put others before herself. I think Jean had a sixth sense for when a family member needed something, and she was always there to provide. One morning I was home helping her to convalesce after a major surgery. Jean was under strict orders from the doctor to limit her activity and was advised not to drive for a while. Well, a call came in from our nephew that he missed the bus and he didn't have a ride to school. Before I could even say,

"Wait, the doctor said to take it easy," Jean flew down the stairs, ran out the door and was in the car. Needless to say, our nephew made it to school on time. Jean put the needs of others before her own. That's what Christ wants us to do for others and for Him. In our weakness...

When we are weak, He is strong. When we turn ourselves over to Him and put others before ourselves, we become strong – for Him and for those we help. It's tough to do, and we can't do it alone. I fail most of the time. I'm guessing that many of us do. However, we're in luck because we're not alone. We have a God who is patient and merciful. He knows the struggles we have and forgives us for our failures.

We also have Jesus with us all the time. By descending in the form of the Holy Spirit to dwell within us, we have a constant companion. If we would only ask, Jesus will help us to let Him lead our lives. If we allow ourselves to be humble and weak, we will become strong because Jesus will occupy a more prominent place in our life – He will become stronger. Seems so simple, right? Actually, it can be if we just say yes to Him.

July 19, 2023

WALKING HUMBLY WITH GOD

If we acknowledge that we can do nothing on our own - or, more importantly, that what we've accomplished in life has happened with the grace of God - we will be more inclined to reach out to help others.

The reading from a recent daily mass was taken from the book of Micah. It closes with the passage, "You have been told, O man, what is good, and what the Lord requires of you: Only to do right and to love goodness, and to walk humbly with your God." (Micah 6:8). In some respects, this passage sums up our entire faith. The first part is self-evident: do right and love goodness. I like the words of the second part even more. They are almost poetic – "walk humbly with your God." The words are directing us to be humble people; these words resonate because that has always been a goal of mine.

This passage also has a bit of legacy in my family. Although it was almost 40 years ago, I still vividly remember my mother quoting this passage when she gave a eulogy for her father. It was quite moving and, as I think about my grandfather, quite accurate. He was a great man – an immigrant from Italy who started with nothing, and over his lifetime, established and built up several businesses that became very successful. Despite his success, he was an understated man. He provided financial help to many fellow immigrants, but he did it in a subtle way and, in many cases, was never paid back. He realized that his success was a gift from God, and he shared that gift with others. And he never acted in a proud manner; he never tried to establish superiority over others. He stayed true to his faith. He walked humbly with his God.

Hearing the passage proclaimed at mass, I reflected on the example my grandfather set with his life, and I experienced a deeper meaning from the words. Firstly, to walk humbly with God means to acknowledge His superiority. He is God. We should believe in Him and praise Him for His goodness to us. Furthermore, to be humble before God is to admit that we need Him. I've heard people say that the biggest sin is pride. If we're proud, we think we can do everything on our own – that we don't need God. It makes sense to me then that pride is called the biggest sin. We turn away from God, and there can't be any bigger sin than that.

I think if we are honest with ourselves – and with God – we'll admit that we let pride get in the way of our relationship with God more often than we realize. I know that's the case with me. It's not intentional. Most of the time I don't even realize that I'm doing it. But that's irrelevant. All that matters is that I'm turning away from God. The opposite of pride is humbleness. Humbleness turns us to God.

If we acknowledge that we can do nothing on our own – or, more importantly, that what we've accomplished in life has happened with the grace of God – we will be more inclined to reach out to help others. If we're not thinking of ourselves first – if we're being humble – our focus will be outward, on those around us. Our humbleness will enable God to work through us to help others.

Humbleness means giving the credit to God for our successes. Humbleness means giving our problems to God, realizing that we can't solve them on our own. Humbleness means considering the needs of others. That's exactly what my grandfather did. He gave credit to God for the blessings he received, and he shared them with others. If we act humbly, God will be with us through whatever challenges we may face.

Referring again to the passage from Micah, focus on the words that follow "walk humbly." The passage implores the reader, "...walk humbly with your God" (emphasis added). If we're walking with God, that means that God is walking with us! Yes, He's God and He reigns supreme. But He humbles Himself to walk with us. God leads by example with His humility. And if we walk humbly with God, He will be at our side as we experience both the joys of our lives as well as the challenges. So, let's strive every day to walk humbly with our God.

July 20, 2022

"I MUST DECREASE"

An action that went completely against conventional wisdom was totally logical to John: He was humbling himself before God and doing His will.

A few days ago (August 29) we celebrated the feast day of St. John the Baptist. He is unique in that he bridged the gap between the Old Testament prophets and Jesus. He went ahead of Jesus and encouraged people to repent so they could be prepared when God – Jesus – came. He was the only prophet who met Jesus. For those reasons, many – perhaps rightly – regard John the Baptist as the greatest prophet. Jesus Himself says this: "I assure you, there is no man born of woman greater than John." (Luke 7:28). But He also says in the very next sentence that the "least born into the kingdom of God is greater than he." (Luke 7:28). Why would Jesus have said this?

We don't have to look much further than John's own words for the answer: "He must increase, while I must decrease." (John 3:30). John's words are remarkable. Here was a man who had incredible popularity. According to the Gospels, large crowds came to the Jordan River to be baptized by him. People hung on his every word, even King Herod. Many were asking if he was the promised Messiah. John's response was an emphatic *"No!"* "He must increase, while I must decrease." At the height of his popularity, John voluntarily took a subordinate role, a back seat to Jesus.

It would be totally counter-cultural today for someone at the height of their popularity/career to fade into the background. I don't think Patrick Mahomes, one of the best quarterbacks in the NFL, would announce that he's going to sit on the bench and let his backup play the next game. Similarly, it's unlikely that a successful CEO in the prime of his/her career would voluntarily agree to step back and let the number two person take over. I wasn't remotely close to that level of success during my career, but I too derived a tremendous amount of satisfaction from having a leadership position, and I was reluctant to give it up.

So why was John so willing to step back? The answer is simple: Because he knew the person who was coming after him was God – God the Son. Furthermore, John knew his role: It was his job to prepare the way for Jesus. He had accomplished his objective, and thus it was time for him to step back. An action that went completely against conventional wisdom was totally logical to John: He was humbling himself before God and doing His will.

Fortunately for us, God is probably not going to ask that we give up our careers to follow Him. But we would do well to follow the example of John the Baptist, even though it goes against our current culture. If we humble ourselves before God and others, God's presence in our lives will increase. In John's case, he stepped back when he had accomplished the plan God had set out for him. In our case, when we step back – when we decrease and let God increase – we will enable God to put into action His plan for us.

Even if the world doesn't appreciate what we're doing, God will, and we in turn will move closer to Him. In doing so, we will create a virtuous circle: As we decrease and move closer to God, we actually increase in God's eyes. "He who humbles himself will be exalted." (Matt 23:12).

September 1, 2022

ONE OF THE CHOSEN

God will be patient with us, and as long as we're trying to do our best, we will be one of His chosen ones, even though we don't deserve it.

"As Jesus was going up to Jerusalem, he took the twelve disciples aside by themselves…" (Matthew 20:17). It's a simple Gospel passage, one that I hadn't paid much attention to in the past. What struck me when I read it today is how pumped the apostles must have been that Jesus chose them to be in His inner circle. They had access to Jesus that no one else had.

We've all had these experiences in our lives. I can remember when I was a young manager at my public accounting firm, the partner asked me to accompany him to the client's board of directors' meeting. This was a Fortune 50 company, and its board was comprised of very senior business and community leaders. There was even a former president of the United States on the board! I was beyond excited. At the meeting, I was given insights into the company and the thought process of its leaders. I also couldn't help but feel pride as well: I had access that few others could get. Over the years, I've attended dozens of client board meetings. If I'm being truthful, the feeling of pride from having that insight and access has never waned.

I think there's little doubt that the apostles felt the same sense of excitement. They probably were saying to themselves, "How special we are!" And that feeling must only have grown after Jesus died and rose from the dead, when they realized that they had been face-to-face with God every day.

Then it hit me. Yes, it certainly had to be an incredible experience for them. But just like I didn't do anything to deserve being invited to my first board meeting, they didn't do anything to warrant their status. They probably weren't any more deserving on their own than any of the other disciples. In fact, they likely didn't do anything to earn their status. Jesus chose them. That's why they became the twelve apostles, plain and simple. Jesus chose twelve very ordinary people – fisherman, tax collectors, etc. – and taught and trained them to be His apostles and start His church. So while they certainly were special, they were special because He chose them.

It's the same with us. We didn't do anything to deserve the incredible mercy that Jesus bestowed on us by giving His life so that we could be forgiven of our sins, and by dwelling within us every moment of our lives. If God gave us what we deserved we would not be very happy at all – at least I know I wouldn't. Instead, He chose us.

He gives every one of us an open invitation – to believe that He is God; that He suffered and died on a cross for us; that He rose so that we could inherit Heaven. He invites us to trust Him and listen to His teachings and strive to do His will. If we do this, we will be saved. It's a guarantee. And when that happens – when we are welcomed into Heaven – we will experience what the apostles experienced when they were with Jesus: the thrill of being face-to-face with

God every day. We each are among God's chosen ones, just like the apostles.

It's quite an amazing thing to say – that we are God's chosen ones. There are times when I feel like I'm doing a good job with my faith. And that makes me think, "Yes, maybe I am one of God's chosen ones." Then, there are times when I don't feel like God's chosen one at all. I'll have one of those days where I don't think I'm doing anything right, and I fall short in my attempts to be close to God. On those days I say to myself, "There's no way I can be one of God's chosen ones."

In fact, neither end of the spectrum is reality. We're all somewhere in the middle, but thanks to God's infinite mercy, we get to share in the inheritance Jesus purchased for us with His life. Again, we didn't earn it. Most of us, like me, are just ordinary people, and we all are sinners.

Even the greatest of the apostles vacillated between these two extremes – in the span of a few hours, no less. At the Last Supper, when Jesus again was telling His apostles what was about to happen to Him and that they too would abandon Him, Peter stood up and boldly proclaimed that even if everyone else left, he would never abandon Jesus. You can almost picture Peter with a proud look as he said this. Then, just a few hours later, after he had denied Jesus three times and saw Jesus turn and look at him, Peter must certainly have felt that he wasn't worthy to be one of His followers.

In fact, neither was true. Peter was special because God chose him, not the other way around. Peter's example should give us hope and inspiration. If he went through the full range of emotions in just a few hours, we shouldn't get flustered when we don't do well in our faith. After all, God made Peter the first pope. God will be patient with us, and as long as we're trying to do our best, we will be one of His chosen ones, even though we don't deserve it.

March 16, 2022

BECOMING MORE LIKE JESUS

Our God also wants us to obey Him. However, He wants us to obey Him not to control us, but so that we can become more like Him, and He can be closer to us.

Last week I missed Sunday mass. I rarely miss Sunday mass. On this particular day we were out of town and had attended a family wedding the night before. I was tired and rationalized that it would be OK this one time. I convinced myself that it wasn't a big deal. I fooled myself into thinking it was fine.

The reality was that I was acting in my own interests. God doesn't require much from us. One thing He does ask is that we spend time with Him each Sunday. By not going to mass I effectively said no to God – I said that I was more important.

In the book of Genesis, we read how the serpent tricked Eve into eating the fruit of the Tree of Knowledge of Good and Evil. He said to Eve "No, God knows well that the moment you eat of it your eyes will be opened and you will be like gods who know what is good and what is bad." (Genesis 3:5). His claim sounded good to Eve, and she gave into the temptation. Her desire to be like a god caused her sin. Adam went right along with Eve for the same reason.

Adam and Eve's actions can seem outlandish to us. It is easy for us to say that we would never do what they did and strive to be a god. However, I think we succumb to this temptation more often than we may care to admit. We may choose to do something because we think it's best for us even though it might hurt someone else. We may decide that one of Jesus' teachings isn't convenient to follow, like not attending mass on a Sunday. Every time we make one of these decisions, we are choosing to disobey God. And if we choose to disobey God, it follows that we're making a decision (even if it's a subconscious one) that we know better than Him – as if we're our own god. Unfortunately, we may not be much different than Adam and Eve.

The temptations of Jesus by the devil stand in sharp contrast to the Genesis story. Jesus had been fasting for 40 days so he was hungry and physically weak. The devil tried to take advantage of the situation by promising him food and other worldly pleasures. Jesus' response provides us a road map for dealing with temptations. He referred to Scripture passages in response to each temptation. (see Matthew, Chapter 4). His responses conformed to the guidance in Scripture, and He obeyed God in each case. He stood His ground and overcame the temptations.

Ultimately, Jesus prevailed because of His obedience. And what happened? His Father sent angels to come and wait on Him (Matthew 4:11), thus providing early proof of His divinity.

In our world, those in positions of authority want people to obey them, often so that they can have control over those people. Our God also wants us to obey Him. However, He wants us to obey Him not to control us, but so that we can become more like Him, and He can be closer to us.

It's another example of the ultimate reversal of conventional wisdom with God. When we disobey God, we are effectively choosing to become our own god, which pulls us away from Him. When we obey Him, we actually become more like Jesus and draw closer to God. And if we try to live our lives in obedience to God, we will make our way to Heaven, whereupon we will be with Jesus and become like Jesus.

February 28, 2023

PAUL E. TUPPER

RECOGNIZING JESUS

That car mechanic who lives next to us? Jesus dwells within him. The math teacher who we see in the grocery store? Jesus dwells within her too.

Have you ever had the experience of running into a childhood acquaintance who turned out completely differently than you ever could have imagined? Perhaps it was the quiet boy from science class who became a famous actor. Or maybe it was the girl who struggled in math class but is now the CEO of a large company. Your immediate reaction might be, "How on Earth did the Johnny I remember become so comfortable in front of people?", or "I never knew Sally was so smart!"

Jesus lived on Earth for about 33 years. He spent 30 of those years in complete obscurity. He lived in the small town of Nazareth and worked as a carpenter. His time in Nazareth was so obscure that we know nothing about it. Nothing is written about this period other than His birth and a few stories from His childhood, such as when His parents found Him in the temple. Jesus spent ninety percent of His life outside of the public eye. His neighbors and friends knew Him as a carpenter and probably thought He would ply His trade as a carpenter in Nazareth for the entirety of His life.

We can imagine, then, their surprise when they heard

what Jesus was doing after He left Nazareth – how He was preaching with authority to massive crowds, how people followed Him wherever He went, how He performed multiple miracles. How can that be, they thought? He was the son of a carpenter. He was a carpenter Himself. He wasn't trained as a rabbi. Where did He gain the authority and knowledge to address all these people, including the elders? It just can't be the same Jesus. There must be some mistake, they no doubt thought.

We've all heard the Gospel passage recounting when Jesus returned to Nazareth and began to teach the people in the synagogue. Their response was, "Where did he get all this? …How is it that such miraculous deeds are accomplished by his hands? Is this not the carpenter, the son of Mary…?" (Mark 5:2-3). In my simple thinking, I've always held these people in contempt for their reaction. I often wondered how they could be so ignorant. Jesus was right in front of them, and they didn't recognize Him.

But if we think about what the His neighbors from Nazareth had observed for thirty years, it's easier to understand the reaction they had. It's not dissimilar from the reaction we might have when we encounter certain childhood acquaintances years later.

To extend the analogy, imagine that you live next to a quiet young man who keeps to himself. You see him in his garage every day working on cars. You think he must be a mechanic. He works long hours and doesn't come out much. He's nice enough, but you don't really get to know him.

Suddenly one day you see him on the television proclaiming that we should repent and return to God.

Large numbers of people are talking about him and following him on social media. What's more, he appears to have supernatural abilities. Some have claimed to see him work miracles. What if this man actually is Jesus living among us?

What would our reaction be? Unfortunately, I fear that my reaction might be similar to that of the people of Nazareth. How could this quiet man who works on cars for a living be able to do this? Where did he get the training for this?

We're not going to encounter Jesus in this way, not like His neighbors in Nazareth did. However, we do encounter Jesus every day. That car mechanic who lives next to us? Jesus dwells within him. The math teacher who we see in the grocery store? Jesus dwells within her too. Do we recognize Him? Or do we react like the people of Nazareth did? Let us not miss the opportunity to encounter Jesus in our everyday lives. Let's remember that Jesus is with us, and let's welcome Him into our hearts by welcoming our neighbors.

November 20, 2023

BEHIND THE SCENES

We don't know what took place during those quiet hours the Apostles had with Jesus. Wouldn't you love to have been a fly on the wall?!

I recently attended a concert that just blew me away. The music, set list, light show and videos combined to produce an incredible performance. We applauded the performers at the end of the show. However, as the stars would be the first to tell you, the show would not have been successful without the great work of the supporting crew – the soundboard team, the light and video technicians, the roadies, etc. What was going on behind the scenes was critical to the show's success.

We see it all the time. At a board meeting, the directors take center stage, but the folks who put together the materials (and, speaking from experience, they can be voluminous!), the schedulers who arrange the various committee meetings that occur around the board meeting and even the food caterers all play a vital role. It's even the case with a small dinner party. Jessica and I hosted another couple for dinner last weekend. We had a great time, and Jessica is the consummate host. However, all the work that we put into making the dinner a success took place beforehand – behind the scenes.

When we think of Jesus and His Apostles, the first

images that come to mind are the major events recorded in the Gospels – e.g., the calling of the disciples, the feeding of the 5,000, the Transfiguration and the like. Jesus was with His Apostles during each of these occasions. However, Jesus spent thousands of hours with them, and there no doubt were many other important events the Apostles witnessed that were not recorded. The vast majority of the time the Apostles spent with Jesus was behind the scenes.

Jesus had several missions to fulfill. He came to preach a message of repentance, encouraging the crowds to turn away from sin and back to the Father. He came to give His life as a sacrifice for us so that we could be saved. He also came to start His Church. Jesus laid the foundation for the Church. However, He needed early leaders who He could trust to build the Church. Those early leaders were the Apostles.

When we start a new role at work, there is a period of training where we learn the skills to apply our new trade. It was the same with Apostles. They needed training. But theirs was no ordinary role. Only Jesus knew how critical their mission was. Accordingly, He planned a significant amount of training – three years' worth. To prepare them for their assignment, Jesus taught them and established deep relationships with each of them. More importantly, by being with them day and night, He provided a living example of how they were to conduct their lives. To ensure the training would be successful, it was important that their environment was free of distractions. It's no surprise, then, that a significant amount of the preparation occurred behind the scenes.

We don't know what took place during those quiet hours

the Apostles had with Jesus. Wouldn't you love to have been a fly on the wall?! We do know that the time clearly was effective – Jesus and His Apostles started a Church that, 2,000 years later, is thriving with hundreds of millions of followers.

We are Jesus' disciples in that Church today. We are supported by our communities within the Church. We need that communal spirit to help us grow as Christians. We need regular Scripture lessons, encouragement from others and the strength we get from receiving the Eucharist regularly. All of these factors help our faith.

But like the Apostles, we also need to be behind the scenes with Jesus. We need time alone with Him to consider the lessons He taught. We need quiet time to contemplate the example He set with His life on Earth. We need time alone with Jesus to be in the moment when He wants to communicate with us. Most importantly, we need behind the scenes time with Jesus to enable the Holy Spirit to come alive within us and guide us on the path Jesus wants us to take.

May 3, 2024

IT'S UP TO US

If we desire to get to Heaven, the process is completely within our control. No one else has a say other than God. If we follow the teachings in the Gospels, God will accept us.

There are certain milestones in our lives that are vitally important to us. Very often such events involve us being chosen for something – i.e., requiring that someone says "yes." Examples could include applying to college or responding to a job posting. These decision points can be life-altering.

Because they are so important to us, we typically put our maximum effort into the process. Think for a minute about the process of applying to school. Our efforts essentially begin at least three years before we fill out the college application form. When we start high school, we work hard to get good grades and take classes that will prepare us for college. We join clubs and play sports. Hopefully, we engage in those activities because we like them, but they also help to buttress our profile for our top college choice. In short, we do everything we can do.

However, the reality is that, despite doing everything possible, we may not be accepted by the school our heart is set on. We may be eminently qualified. But the decision is not completely within our control. For reasons we don't understand, we may not be accepted. Why? Because we're competing with others, and someone else is making the decision.

It can be the same when applying for a job. During our careers, we focus on building up our CV's. We strive to obtain a variety of experiences in our jobs, we continuously look to enhance our skills and we fill out our profiles with multiple activities, like community service. At some point an opening may come up for the job we've always desired. We have spent years preparing ourselves for the opportunity. When it arises, we work tirelessly on the application and prepare for the interview. We may be an extremely qualified candidate, and we really, really want the job. However, the decision is not within our control, and for reasons no one can explain, there is a possibility we may not be accepted.

As Christians, there is something else in our lives that is – or at least should be – vitally important to us: being faithful followers of Jesus. We strive to live good lives, Christian lives. We want Jesus to approve of us and hope that He will deem us worthy to enter Heaven when our time on Earth is complete. We are taught about Heaven by our parents from our youngest days. As we grow up, we learn from teachers and religious leaders what we need to do to reach Heaven. Most importantly, we are taught by Jesus Himself. The Gospels provide all the information we need to help us conduct ourselves in a way worthy of being called Christians.

It might be beneficial if we think of our spiritual journey in the same manner that we approach a college application or job interview. If we do, we would spend time preparing.

We would do the things that would help put us in the best position to be successful. We would put all our efforts into the process. There is a big difference, however, between applying for a job and striving for Heaven. When applying for a job, we can be a qualified candidate and still not get the job. Ultimately, it's not up to us.

When it comes to Heaven, if God deems us qualified, we get in. Period. There is no competition with others. There is no quota on the number of us that can go to Heaven. There is room for everyone. And what's more, we don't have to be perfect. That's good because none of us ever will be. We can and will make mistakes. But we have a God who is merciful and is ready to forgive us every time we stray from Him. He gives us a second chance – over and over. Can you imagine if we had a second chance at that dream job or top college?

Being a Christian may not be easy. However, the Gospels give us guidance on exactly what we need to do. If we desire to get to Heaven, the process is completely within our control. No one else has a say other than God. If we follow the teachings in the Gospels, God will accept us. So, in the end, it's up to us to say "yes" to the teachings of the Gospels – and "yes" to God.

October 2, 2023

CO-HEIRS?

Although He is God and we are sinners, God, through His Son, has extended us an invitation to be co-heirs of His Kingdom with Jesus.

Have you ever been given something that maybe you didn't think you deserved? An opportunity just falls into your lap and you're not sure how or why.

One day, in the midst of a crazy stretch of meetings, I received a call from the vice chair of our Audit practice in my firm. After a bit of small talk, he asked me if I would consider becoming the lead partner for one of our largest clients. It was a prestigious role, and one that could be career-defining as well.

I had previously worked on the engagement team for this client as a young partner, but really had never conceived of being the overall partner in charge of the account. As the years went by, I had taken on more challenging roles and felt that my career was proceeding well. However, the call from the vice chair surprised me. While this was a role that many in the firm probably aspired to, I hadn't thought it would be a possibility for me. It came out of the blue.

But it didn't take me long to answer him. Of course I

would love to take on the role! It would be the most challenging engagement of my professional life. How could I say no? That call changed the trajectory of my career.

I realize that not everyone is lucky enough to receive such a call and opportunity that could boost a career. However, each of us has received a much more important call – one that can change the direction of our entire life. We have been called by Jesus. If we say "yes," He will be with us every day, from now to eternity. Jesus has called us to be His children. In the words of St. Paul, "The Spirit himself gives witness with our spirit that we are children of God. But if we are children, we are heirs as well: heirs of God, heirs with Christ…" (Romans 8:16-17).

Talk about receiving something we don't deserve! It doesn't matter who we are or what we have done/not done. We all are invited to be co-heirs with Christ.

Most of us try to live good lives. We strive to be faithful to the teachings of Jesus. However, we fail often. We're sinners, and we can't change on our own. Thankfully, Jesus took care of that for us. By dying on the Cross, He saved us. Our God is a loving God, and by putting our sins on the shoulders of His Son, He showed us the depth of that love.

But amazingly, God didn't stop there. He not only saved us, but He wants us to be with Him forever. Although He is God and we are sinners, God, through His Son, has extended us an invitation to be co-heirs of His Kingdom with Jesus.

We each have received a "phone call" with the most incredible offer – one that sounds too good to be true. Except that it's not.

With His call, Jesus has invited us to let Him live within us. He has offered to give us His Spirit to dwell in us. The Spirit that St. Paul referred to will be our constant companion in good times and in difficult times. That Spirit will guide us when we need direction. That Spirit will help protect us from the temptations of the evil one. That same Spirit will lead us to our inheritance.

What are we expected to do in return? When I said yes to the offer from the vice chair of my firm, I was ecstatic, but I knew I would work extremely hard for the following years.

On the contrary, when we say yes to Jesus, He does most of the work. In fact, He already did the hard work two thousand years ago. We do have responsibilities, though. We must be faithful to Him. We must put Him first. And by putting Him first, we must allow Him to lead the way for us. It won't always be easy. There will be challenges and there will be temptations. There will be times of suffering, but if we remain faithful, we will win the prize in the end. St. Paul promises that we are heirs with Christ, "if only we suffer with him so as to be glorified with him." (Romans 8:17).

Could it really be that we, sinners though we are, have been invited to be co-heirs with Jesus and inherit His kingdom? You better believe it! How can we say no?

July 24, 2024

ALLOWING GOD TO INFLUENCE US

God doesn't expect us to accomplish His will all on our own. He's there constantly to provide help, whenever we ask for it.

I am a firm believer that God doesn't dictate everything that happens in our lives. He allows human nature to take its course. However, I believe God can and does choose to intervene in certain situations, particularly when our hearts and minds are focused on Him.

Oftentimes, I'll be thinking about something as I'm saying my prayers, and right afterward that same thought will come up in the daily Scripture reading, the priest's homily at mass or in a spiritual book. It happens relatively frequently. In fact, it happened today. I spent a lot of time during my morning prayer talking to God about everything that was on my mind. In the midst of my various thoughts, a concept popped into my head that God seems to be calling me to be a witness to Him by writing about my experiences and my faith journey. I hadn't thought about this concept recently, so I reflected upon it for a while, wanting to better discern what God is looking for from me.

Shortly after I finished my prayers, I read the daily reflection in the books that I typically read each day. In the book *Jesus Always* by Sarah Young, the final paragraph for the day's reflection was: "To acclaim Me also means to acknowledge My excellence publicly. *You are the light of the world* because you know Me as your Savior-God. I want you to *let your light shine before men*; tell them the wonders of who I am – and all I have done. *Proclaim the excellencies of Him who called you out of darkness into His marvelous Light.*" (*Jesus Always*, p 208). [Italics appear in her book to reference biblical quotes.]

I don't believe in coincidences, especially when it comes to God. Today, I believe that God put the thought into my head before reading the daily reflection in order to amplify His message to me. As my experience illustrates, God can influence our thoughts and what we do, especially if we take the time to be in His presence, talk to Him or just spend a quiet moment with Him.

God truly accomplishes amazing things in our lives and through our lives. Sometimes it may seem difficult to live the life that God desires. Fortunately for us, God knew that in advance, before He even created us. He knows our weaknesses, and He loves us not in spite of them but because of them. As a result, God doesn't expect us to accomplish His will all on our own. He's there constantly to provide help, whenever we ask for it. All we need to do to accomplish God's will is to have the desire for a close personal relationship with Him and to devote the time to be with Him and let Him communicate with us. After all, He dwells within us through His Holy Spirit. He's right there – within us – whenever we need Him.

Post-script:

It's now late 2023, and I've been writing for almost two years. Today, I was looking back on my old notebooks and came across the above reflection. I remember well the experience I wrote about. In the weeks leading up to it, I had been spending more time trying to discern God's plan for me. In the process, I had essentially kept a journal documenting my thoughts. While I was generally heading in the direction of starting to write for God, it wasn't until this experience that I progressed from the thinking phase to the execution phase. "Allowing God to Influence Us" was my first reflection! God patiently guided me, and eventually I received His message and understood His calling for me. It took a while, but I had allowed God to influence me.

July 17, 2021

JUST BE WILLING

...one thing I am certain of: If we're willing to listen to God and follow His plan, He will lead us to what He desires for us.

Ever since I retired from my job as an accountant (almost two years ago), I've spent a lot of time attempting to discern God's will for me. Based on His promptings, I know that spiritual writing is one of the ministries God has called me to do. Whether that's the endgame or an interim step in His ultimate plan for me, I don't know. However, I do know that as long as I continue to write, I will be carrying out His plan.

Notwithstanding this, I often become disappointed in myself because I don't make time every day to write a reflection. It's certainly my goal, but I'm not always successful. On some days I have commitments and I run out of time. On other days I don't feel any inspiration. On still others I'm just lazy, to be honest. It's something I pray about often, asking Jesus to help me be more dedicated.

I also occasionally wonder whether God is calling me to do more than to just write – e.g., engage in volunteer work. As I think about this, I inevitably say to myself: "What skills do I have? What can I really do to help?" Today, as I was reflecting on what to write, I came across a page I had ripped out of last month's *The Word Among Us*. The subject of the particular passage was how we can use our skills to serve God by helping others. The author mentioned that we often have a tendency to separate our spiritual lives from our skills or hobbies. He suggested that maybe Jesus wants us to use our skills or hobbies to accomplish His plan. The author then used an example that I found remarkable: "For example, He might use your ... knack for accounting to help launch a new ministry." (*The Word Among Us*, May 26, 2022). I never contemplated that the skillset I had spent 30-plus years developing might just be one that God plans to put to use.

That certainly hit home for me. I'm still not sure what God has in store for me, but this passage helped me realize that it's possible that He may want me to use my accounting skills in some fashion as part of His plan. Maybe He wants me to use them in a direct way, such as helping people manage their personal finances. Or perhaps God plans to work in a more indirect way. For instance, maybe the audience God intends for me to reach through my writing are people like me, so having a background in accounting will help provide context.

Either way, the message I can take from the passage is not to worry about whether I have the skills to accomplish what God is asking, but rather to trust that God will provide what I need. Incidentally, that applies to my writing as well, as I often second-guess my abilities. Rather than second-guessing ourselves, I – and we – just need to be willing to respond to the need and God's related call when it arises.

When will we know when God is calling us to a ministry? I think He will nudge us. Last summer, during a period when I was spending relatively more quiet time with Him, I felt God say to me during my daily walk, "Be alert." So I try to be alert. It requires some focus and carving out time to be alone with God, disciplines that I'm not always very good at doing. But one thing I am certain of: If we're willing to listen to God and follow His plan, He will lead us to what He desires for us. Furthermore, if we're carrying out God's plan, there is no need for us to question whether we have the requisite skills. We can trust that God will provide us what we need. All it takes on our part is to be willing. God will take care of the rest.

June 8, 2022

MANAGING EXPECTATIONS

...just like most of us won't climb up the corporate ladder in a week, our faith is not going to be perfected quickly either. It's not going to be instantaneous.

We live in a world where it seems everything is exaggerated. It seems people want the best of everything. Everyone wants to live in a big house. We want the best job and to advance up the career ladder as quickly as possible. We also live in a world of instant gratification. We expect to be rewarded for our successes, and it's become commonplace to post those successes on social media so others can see them. Unfortunately, reality often differs from our perceptions. We would do well to manage our expectations.

I think many of us have the same mindset with our spiritual lives – at least I do. When I spend time working on my faith – whether it's alone with God or doing something to help others – I often experience a great feeling of contentment. I think that God must be happy with me and that everything's going to be perfect from here on out. My faith will continue to grow stronger and I'll be happier, right?

In point of fact, if we invest more and more time in our

relationship with God, our faith *will* grow, and we *will* be happier. But just like most of us won't climb up the corporate ladder in a week, our faith is not going to be perfected quickly either. It's not going to be instantaneous. In rare circumstances perhaps it will; however, it's highly unlikely that we will have an immediate conversion like St. Paul had on his way to Damascus. It's much more likely to be small and gradual. And that's ok.

We may not feel any different day to day, and we probably won't think differently on a conscious level, but it's important not to fall into the trap of thinking that there's not a change happening within us. In most cases, God wants us to take small steps. For many of us, certainly me, that's probably all we can handle.

Over a year ago, I took the step of saying yes to God – yes, I would live my life according to His will and put Him first. I expected everything to be different after that. As I look back on it, I guess in the short term things were different, in the sense that I really felt great and I tried to be more focused on my spiritual life. Over time though, by any conventional measure, I haven't lived up to the commitment I made that day.

I think, however, that my situation is a perfect illustration of why God wants us to take small steps. Simply put, most of us – certainly I – wouldn't be able to handle an instantaneous, complete conversion to God. God wants us to put Him first, and He wants us to be devoted to Him, but He also knows the weakness of our human nature. Accordingly, He guides us with small steps – steps that will help us to get stronger over time.

When I look back over the past year, I certainly can see

that I've taken several steps forward, even if they're small steps. I'm going to daily mass more frequently. I'm writing with greater regularity. I think I'm doing a better job of giving my time when those around me need it. Without question, I've had countless shortfalls as well, the most notable being that I'm not consistently putting God first. However, when I think of the small steps that I have made over the year, I can see definite progress. I'm not yet living my life for Jesus, but I'm a little closer to that goal than I was a year ago. I'm sure if each of us were to stop and look back over the past few months or years, we would have the same reaction.

So instead of expecting instant gratification and immediate success in our relationship with God, let's remember to manage our expectations. Let's take note of the progress we have made and keep moving forward. And we should make time to celebrate the little steps we are taking. After all, every one of those steps gets us closer to our final destination.

October 5, 2022

IT'S WHERE YOU FINISH

When we recognize our failures, and turn back to Him with a sincere heart, He will welcome us back. Every time.

My son Paul got off the line a bit slowly. It took a few steps before he was in rhythm. But boy, once he was, it looked like he had been shot out of a cannon. Paul was running the 60-yard dash at a college baseball camp. Speed was one of the key attributes the college scouts were looking for, and the 60 was how they measured it.

Because of his start, Paul was running behind his competitor. However, once he got in stride, he literally blew past the other guy and finished with one of the best times among the several hundred athletes attending the camp. The result put Paul on the scouts' radar.

The pattern repeated itself over and over. Paul ran dozens of 60s as he competed for a spot on a college baseball team. Every time he started slow, and every time he clocked one of the fastest runs. Ultimately, he did receive an invitation to play for a college team, and his speed was a contributor. It's not where you start, it's where you finish.

This adage applies to situations beyond sports as well. I started rather slowly in my job. It took a bit for me to get into my groove. Meanwhile, many colleagues were racing past me. Some left the firm for much higher paying jobs. I didn't worry about what others were doing, but rather focused on continually improving. I stayed with it and eventually had a rewarding career.

The same can be said for my faith. I most definitely started slowly. Sure, I did the basics: I attended Sunday mass, I prayed every day, but I didn't invest the time to develop a personal relationship with Jesus. I thought I was advancing my faith, but the truth is I was treading water while my focus was on my job and my family. I still have plenty of days when I "start slowly."

Fortunately for us, our God is endlessly patient and gives us plenty of chances to get into our stride – to turn back to Him. Jesus' last act before He died tells us everything we need to know about God's mercy. As He hung on the cross in absolute agony, the man being crucified next to Him pleaded: "Jesus, remember me when you enter upon your reign." (Luke 23:42). We know next to nothing about this man. We don't know if he had been a believer in Jesus, but I'm guessing he was not. What we know is he was a criminal and he was crucified. That he was put to the cross would imply that he must have done something bad, so I don't think it's likely he was a faith-filled person. However, as he was dying, he realized this man next to him was different. He experienced a conversion and pleaded for mercy.

Jesus' response was extraordinary. "I assure you: This day you will be with me in paradise." (Luke 23:43). How could Jesus say this? Here was a man who deserved his fate. He even said so to his fellow criminal (v. 41). So how on earth did he have the gall to ask Jesus, a totally innocent man, for mercy? And how on earth could Jesus have said anything other than leave me alone?

However, Jesus showed mercy, incredible mercy. And that mercy made this common criminal the first person Jesus took to Heaven. Jesus didn't say He would think about it or maybe He would remember the man in a few years. No. Jesus assured him he would be with Jesus that very day.

That same mercy opened up the gates of Heaven for us as well. We should want to spend our lives glorifying God for His love for us. We should strive to be good Christians all the time. But we know that's not always going to happen. We know we will make mistakes. We may get off to a slow start. There will be times when we don't spend enough time with our faith, times when we will be treading water.

Fortunately, God knows it too. But, if we keep running our race, if we persevere in our faith, we will prevail, thanks to God. When we recognize our failures, and turn back to Him with a sincere heart, He will welcome us back. Every time. It's not where you start, it's where you finish.

September 13, 2024

LISTENING FOR JESUS

By telling me He loves me, Jesus was reminding me to put things into His hands, to trust Him, and maybe above all, to always be thankful – thankful for His love that is so strong He was willing to suffer and die for us.

I was looking back over some of my journal entries today, and I came across a Post-it note from September of last year. At that time, I had started to make a more concerted effort to spend quiet time each day and listen to Jesus. I've mentioned previously that I have not been very successful at trying to do this on a consistent basis, but last year I got off to a good start. The Post-it contained the words I heard from Jesus while I was being quiet.

Incidentally, the first such instance occurred while I was on the train coming home from New York City, which proves that you can find quiet time almost anywhere – as long as you're willing to slow everything down for a time and listen.

On September 22, 2021, Jesus' first words to me were as follows:

"I love you."

"Do you know that I love you?"

"You are not alone."

"Start to organize your writings."

"That's enough for tonight."

Then, on September 23rd, I heard Jesus say again "I love you."

As I looked back on my notes, my first thought was I was extremely happy that I had taken the time to write down what I had heard. I sometimes can be a procrastinator and then become forgetful, but thankfully, this was not one of those times. Secondly, I was struck by the first words Jesus said to me after I finally had consciously taken time to be quiet and listen: "I love you."

I was expecting to hear something like "I want you to help your relatives more" or "I want you to spend more time volunteering." Both of those instructions would have been on point. However, Jesus didn't say anything like that. What He said was, "I love you." Then Jesus repeated it in the form of a question: "Do you know that I love you?" Moreover, on the second day, He said it again! It's clear that He was trying to send me a message.

If you were to have asked me on September 21, 2021, "Paul, do you think Jesus loves you?", I undoubtedly would have said yes. So why was Jesus telling me something I already knew? I think it's because I did not – and probably still do not – comprehend the depth of His love for me, His love for each of us. I had gone through a brutal experience and had suffered an enormous loss, and Jesus was there for me. He got me through it. In fact, He's always there, but we don't always acknowledge or remember it.

We often are too quick to turn inward when things get tough instead of turning to Jesus. By telling me He loves me,

Jesus was reminding me to put things into His hands, to trust Him, and maybe above all, to always be thankful – thankful for His love that is so strong He was willing to suffer and die for us. Lastly, maybe it was to encourage me to be open to His plan for me. If Jesus loves us so much, wouldn't we want to carry out His plan? It's the least we can do, right?

Incidentally, His words, "You are not alone," also were prescient. At the time, I interpreted them to mean that I wasn't alone because Jesus is always with me, dwelling in me through His Holy Spirit. And that's definitely true. But as I soon realized, there was more to His message. Jesus spoke those words to me on September 22. Just a few days later, I saw Jessica for the second time. As you will read in the next reflection ("So Grateful"), Jesus' words to me were fulfilled.

The bottom line is that if we take time to be with Jesus, and especially, to listen, we will not be disappointed. Jesus will speak to us – maybe not every time, but He will speak to us. And we can be sure that His message will be transformative for us.

June 29, 2022

SO GRATEFUL

I did nothing to deserve these blessings, just like we do nothing to deserve the many gifts God bestows on us... They are gifts from God, and we should cherish them every day.

We just celebrated Valentine's Day, where we take time to let that special someone know how much they mean to us. I was no exception. Jessica, my better half (and she truly is my better half) and I spent a quiet evening at home. She made a delicious dinner and surprised me with my two favorite desserts from the local Italian bakery. She already has my heart completely, but she put it over the top with those desserts! It was a perfect evening.

When I think of the past several years of my life, occasions like Valentine's Day make me appreciative of how God has taken care of me.

I was married for over 25 years and thus had celebrated many Valentine's Days. I had never stopped to think that such celebrations might end. Then, in September of 2018, my wife Jean was diagnosed with cancer. I never stopped believing that God would heal her, and Jean never stopped fighting. However, in August of 2019, God called Jean back home.

I don't really remember Valentine's Day in 2020 and 2021. That's probably not by accident. I'm guessing my mind blocked those memories. What I do remember was feeling down in the dumps and wishing the day would pass quickly. But I knew I had to move forward and cope. With God's help, I was able to figure out a way to do that. I spent a lot of time on spiritual activities during those first two years after Jean's death – praying, reading, reflecting, writing, etc. With God's help I was, in fact, moving forward. However, I still felt a void.

I frequently talked to God about what I was feeling during the summer of 2021. I expressed my loneliness and asked God for His help. I tried to commit to Him that, if it was His will that I be alone, I would accept it. Notice the word "tried" in the previous sentence. I really did want to do God's will but, in fact, it was hard to commit to being alone. I said it, but I really hoped that it was not God's plan for me.

Less than two months after these conversations with God, Jean's sister suggested that she and I have dinner with a long-time friend of hers. This friend had experienced a similar loss around the same time as I had. I said, "Sure," not really knowing why I had agreed. I found out later it was the same for her friend – she vacillated but agreed to the dinner. We met and had a really nice time. Six months later, Jessica and I celebrated Valentine's Day. We've been together for over a year now, and two days ago we celebrated our second Valentine's together.

Having experienced God's mercy and His love firsthand, it's not possible to overstate it. God pulled me close to Him after Jean died, and His compassion and His grace got me through a brutal time, enabling me to turn forward. But things still weren't completely right, and God knew it. As I was starting to struggle again, He brought someone new into my life. It didn't take long for me to realize that Jessica is the person I want to spend the rest of my life with. Rather than give examples as to why, I can sum it up with the words my niece said after seeing us together for the first time: "He's acting like the old Paul again!" The positive change is because God answered my prayers and brought Jessica into my life.

I was incredibly blessed to have had Jean in my life for so many years, and now I'm incredibly blessed again to have Jessica for, God willing, the rest of my life. I did nothing to deserve these blessings, just like we do nothing to deserve the many gifts God bestows on us -- most importantly the redemption that Christ purchased for each of us by His own body. They are gifts from God, and we should cherish them every day.

February 16, 2023

WE ARE GIFTS

I fall short so often in my faith, but Jesus not only tolerates me, He cherishes me. He cherishes us. I am a gift to Him; we are gifts to <u>Him</u>!

Everyone loves gifts. When someone takes the time to pick out something for me, I'm grateful. It makes me feel special. Moreover, when someone tells me that I am a gift to them, I am overjoyed. It's a great feeling to know that we are important to someone else, especially someone we care about.

The Gospel reading from this past Sunday (John 17) is one of my favorites: "And I have given them the glory you gave me, so that they may be one, as we are one, I in them and you in me…" (John 17:21-23) With these words, Jesus is binding us together – with Him, with His Father and with each other. In these words, Jesus is also again foretelling His disciples that He will always be with them ("I in them"). And He makes the same promise to us. In fact, His promise has already been fulfilled – that first Pentecost Sunday, when God sent the Holy Spirit to dwell within us.

I've read this passage many times. I mentioned that it's one of my favorite passages in the Gospels. Jean and I used it for our wedding mass, so I'm very familiar with it. However, this time, the words really spoke to me. Jesus is telling His disciples – and us – that He will return and dwell within us. And, if we embrace that Jesus dwells within us, the next passage in this Gospel reading in turn will be fulfilled: "... that their unity may be complete." (John 17:23)

The ensuing verses amplify the depth of Jesus' love for His disciples and us: "Father, they are your gift to me. I wish that where I am, they also may be with me..." (John17:24-25). We know that Jesus lowered Himself to become like us, live among us and suffer and die so we could be saved. That makes Him a gift to us, right? That's definitely true.

But we are a gift to Him? How can we be a gift to God the Son, the one who saved us? Yet here is Jesus, thanking His Father that He gave us to Him. How do we feel when we receive a gift? We're happy. How do we feel when we receive a gift that we really love? We cherish it. We already know that Jesus loves us – He died for us. If we are a gift to Jesus, that means He cherishes us! Can you imagine that? I fall short so often in my faith, but Jesus not only tolerates me, He cherishes me. He cherishes us. I am a gift to Him; we are gifts to <u>Him</u>! It's almost too good to be true. In fact, it would be too good to be true if it hadn't come from God.

But Jesus doesn't stop there. He loves us so much – He cherishes His Father's gift so much—that He asks His Father to bring us to where He is. Jesus wants us to be with Him forever. And the Father answered His Son's prayer. He sent Jesus to dwell within us through the Holy Spirit ("I in them"). So often God blesses us when we don't deserve it. We are sinners, but Jesus gave His life to open the gates of Heaven for us. He then came back to live within us and show us the way to those gates – His Holy Spirit is our GPS to Heaven – all because we are a gift to Him. He doesn't want to lose any of us. We are gifts to our Savior who gave Himself for us.

May 31, 2022

BE PATIENT

I can't be in a rush when I pray, worrying about getting onto the next task after I'm finished with my prayers. While I don't think God expects me, or any of us, to spend the whole day in prayer, He desires me to be focused on Him when I do pray...

I tend to be in a rush all the time. It no doubt started early in my career as an accountant, where there was always a long list of things to do. In response, I learned to be efficient. In fact, I prided myself on being efficient! That desire spilled over into my home life. It was important to get the weekend chores done as quickly as possible so I could have some time to relax. The problem - which I didn't understand at the time - was that it's impossible to relax when you have this mindset. I've been retired for almost a year now and am still trying to "rewire" myself. One of my frequent prayers to God is to help me with this.

The past several months have been fulfilling in the development of my relationship with Jesus. I feel like I'm starting to get an understanding - still quite preliminary - of what it means to have a personal relationship with Him. But the more I understand, the more I realize how far there is to go. Then I start to think that I've been at this for a few months now; why haven't I made more progress? I said "yes" to God but still haven't been able to let go of everything for Him. What's the matter with me? I'm spending more time each day in prayer, reflection, writing, reading, attending mass. Why am I not making better progress?

I think God's response is "be patient." As opposed to tackling my to-do list at work, speed and efficiency are not relevant in my faith and my relationship with Jesus. In fact, it's just the opposite. It's important to give it time and turn everything over to God. If I trust in Him, He will continue to develop my faith according to His plan. Father Louis Lallemant noted, "When souls have abandoned themselves to be led by the Holy Spirit, he raises them <u>little by little</u> (emphasis added) and guides them. At the beginning, these souls do not know where they are being led, but <u>little by little</u> (emphasis added again), a light shines within and makes them see all their actions and the guidance of God on their actions..." (*In the School of the Holy Spirit*, p. 70; Jacques Philippe).

So the process of conversion will take time. In my case, it's important to be patient in both the micro and macro aspects. For the micro, I can't be in a rush when I pray, worrying about getting onto the next task after I'm finished with my prayers. While I don't think God expects me, or any of us, to spend the whole day in prayer, He desires me to be focused on Him when I do pray, and it's hard to be focused on Him when I'm worrying about something else. Regarding the macro, I need to be focused on being in the moment with Christ, and I should not be trying to evaluate how much progress I might be making in my goal of being closer to Jesus. If I live with Jesus each day and let God carry out His plan, I WILL make progress. And so my prayer to God to re-wire me isn't just for the purpose of helping me to transition to retirement. There is a much more important reason to pray for the grace to slow things down: It's necessary if I'm going to grow closer to Jesus.

In the midst of the ever-increasing pace of our lives, it would be good for all of us to slow things down, even if just for a few moments. It sounds ironic, but the faster our lives get, the more important it is to slow down. Take a few moments each day and live in the moment with Jesus. And, little by little, God's light will shine within us and lead us forward according to His will.

September 21, 2021

OUR DESERT PLACE

We need time alone for prayer, for recharging, for time with God. Just like being with His Father strengthened Jesus, being with Jesus will strengthen us for the journey ahead.

We were wrapping up the audit, and I was about to present the findings to the Audit Committee. The client was one of the largest and most diversified public companies in the world and this would be the first time I was presenting to them. The Committee was a who's-who of former CEOs of Fortune 50 companies. I had spent a year attending the Audit Committee meetings, shadowing my predecessor, but this would be the first time that I actually would be taking center stage. Presenters had to stand in the front of the room and talk without any notes or other aids. To say I was nervous would be a vast understatement!

I spent hours preparing. Undoubtedly, I tormented my team with requests for supporting information. Looking back at that experience 20 years ago, one aspect of the preparation stands out. In the days leading up to the meeting, I sequestered myself for a period each day. It was important to have time alone to get my thoughts together, to practice the presentation, to calm myself, to get mentally and emotionally ready. The daily drive home was the perfect setting. I was in my car, totally alone, and it was late so there were no other cars on the road. It was my quiet place. In the car, I got myself ready for the biggest challenge of my career to that point.

In yesterday's Gospel, Jesus instructs the Apostles, "Come away by yourselves to a deserted place and rest a while." (Mark 6:30). The Apostles were no different from us. They had a monumental challenge ahead of them. Jesus had chosen them to spread His Word and start the Church. They would face fierce resistance. He had given them a taste of it by sending them out in pairs to proclaim the Good News. They had just returned and were tired. To prepare them for the road ahead, He told them to rest.

Jesus practiced the same routine Himself. Before any major event, He went off to a deserted place to pray to His Father – alone. There are numerous examples in the Gospels. Jesus went to the desert to fast and pray for 40 days before He started His public ministry. Early in that ministry, just as Jesus was becoming popular and drawing huge crowds, He withdrew to be with His Father. Mark tells us, "Rising early the next morning, he went off to a lonely place in the desert; there he was absorbed in prayer." (Mark 1:35). And, of course, after the Last Supper, Jesus went to the Garden of Gethsemane to pray and draw strength for what lied ahead for Him.

Like Jesus and like the Apostles, we need our time in the desert. We need it before major challenges in our work or home life. Importantly, we need it in our spiritual lives. Just like my routine before that Audit Committee meeting, when we're facing a big challenge most of us probably go to our quiet places without even thinking about it. It occurs innately. However, I'm not sure it always happens naturally on the spiritual front – at least I know it doesn't with me.

Unlike the critical events in our temporal lives, we may not encounter a spiritual crisis that seemingly requires all our energy. However, we are in the battle of our spiritual lives every day. Satan is conniving to steal us away from God, and we need to be strong to resist him. There will be times when our defenses are down. It may be that we're tired from a long stretch at work. Perhaps a loved one has been battling a severe illness and it's worn us down with anxiety. Or maybe we have become lukewarm in our faith. We're just not feeling it – we've gone into the dreaded and insidious "drift."

In those times, we must head to our desert. We need time alone for prayer, for recharging, for time with God. Just like being with His Father strengthened Jesus, being with Jesus will strengthen us for the journey ahead. We must seek His presence. We can't do it alone. One way to ensure we have that strength is to go to our quiet place daily, even if it's just for a few minutes. But we need to make the conscious decision to spend time in our desert.

The time I spent on the ride home all those years ago prepared me for the Audit Committee meeting. To be honest I was still a bit nervous when I walked into the Board room. However, the presentation went well thanks to my desert time.

Similarly, our time each day with Jesus will bear fruit. We will emerge from our desert strengthened and refreshed, ready to face whatever life throws at us.

July 22, 2024

TRYING TOO HARD

...while it's okay ⁃ and actually good ⁃ to set high expectations, it's also okay ⁃ and actually better ⁃ to manage those expectations: in our daily activities, our careers, our relationships with others and in our relationship with God.

I set high expectations for myself. I try to be at my best all the time and become frustrated when I fall short. Of course, it's not realistic to think we'll be at our best at all times – that we'll always be "on." Yet, I become disappointed when I fall short, which not surprisingly, is often. This applies to my temporal life as well as my spiritual life. Every morning my first prayer is, "Jesus, help me to perform at a high level today for You."

It's certainly good to set high expectations for ourselves. But it is counter-productive to get frustrated every time we fall short. I can't be sure, but in the spiritual realm, it might even be a sin because this type of thinking takes our focus away from God and puts it on ourselves.

Yesterday, when I was with Jessica, I fell short of my expectations of how I should be when we're together. At times, I was thinking about things that I needed to do, so I wasn't totally present, totally in the moment with her. I realized what I had been doing, got frustrated with myself and apologized. Instead of being upset with me, Jessica had a somewhat remarkable reaction. She said, "Paul, you're being too hard on yourself. Everything is fine."

Today on my way into church for daily mass, I was feeling badly about where I was at that moment in my relationship with Jesus. Frequently, it feels like I'm falling short in my relationship with Him. In fact there's no doubt that I'm falling short. But just like Jessica's response, Jesus' message to me was remarkable. As soon as I started to get frustrated with myself, I heard the following words, "Paul, you're being too hard on yourself." I have no doubt that it was Jesus speaking to me through His Holy Spirit.

Think about it. This is our God, whose Son suffered and died so that we could be freed from our sins; the One who is always with us through His Holy Spirit; the One who desires nothing more than for us to have a personal relationship with Him. He's not asking for much, especially given all that He did and does for us. And yet, His response to my falling short is, "You're being too hard on yourself?" Only God, whose love for us is clearly unfathomable to our human minds and whose mercy and compassion is equally boundless, could have such a response.

Jesus' response, as well as Jessica's, left an impression on me. I realized that while it's okay – and actually good – to set high expectations, it's also okay – and actually better – to manage those expectations: in our daily activities, our careers, our relationships with others and in our relationship with God.

Maybe the best approach is to start each day with the goal of being the best we can be, but at the same time realize that we're not going to achieve this goal every day. In fact, we may fail to achieve it most of the time. However, as long as we're trying to be our best, that's going to be okay with those who love us and especially with God. He's always going to love us.

March 4, 2022

GOD'S PLAN

We each have been called to minister for God. Rather than giving in to our fears of stepping out of our comfort zone, let's put ourselves in God's hands and trust Him.

Shortly after I retired I would say the following prayer every day:

"God, please give me the wisdom to discern Your will and the courage to carry it out."

I haven't said that prayer in a while, but it came back to me today while I was praying the Rosary. As with everything associated with God, the timing was not an accident. Lately I've been spending more time thinking about my understanding that God is calling me to be a witness to Him, presumably through my writing. Momentum in this area has also been picking up. I've gotten several signals from God asking me to write. Jessica has been pushing me to write more frequently. Recently I decided to write at least a little bit every day during Lent this year. My sense is that God wants me to take the next step and start to share my witness of Him with others. And, to be honest, that scares me.

Both Jessica and my sister have been a constant source of encouragement. And I am feeling more momentum regarding writing. I'm excited, but I'm also scared. I know

God will help me. After all, this is what He wants me to do, right? But then the questions start: "Who would want to hear from me?" "What do I have to offer?" Also, I've lived my adult life with the mindset of trying to fly below the radar. I don't like to draw attention to myself. Furthermore, I've generally been very private about my faith. Finally, I don't know exactly what to do in terms of the next step.

I believe that's why the Holy Spirit reminded me of my little prayer today. I'm clearly going to be stepping out of my comfort zone as I move forward, so I'm going to need courage – a lot of it. And, despite all my misgivings, the irony is that I know I'm going to get that courage from God.

Jesus showed us the ultimate in courage through His passion and death, which He willingly endured for us. His Father gave Him the strength to face His trials. Whatever it is that I will need to fulfill God's plan, I'm confident that God will provide it. He will give me courage and strength and whatever else is necessary. In fact, the reality is that I already have it – His Son dwells within me, and He is the source of all my strength. He dwells within all of us. I know this, but I still get scared.

As I reflect on the next steps that I might soon take – whatever they may be – I need to remember to put myself in God's hands and trust in Him. We each have been called to minister for God. Rather than giving in to our fears of stepping out of our comfort zone, let's put ourselves in God's hands and trust Him. Or, following one of the principles that I recite every morning, "Let go, let God." Let God take our ministries wherever He wants them to go and not worry about what might happen or what others may think.

Easier said than done? Actually, it is easy. I can accomplish God's will – we all can accomplish God's will -- with His help and the with encouragement of those who mean the most to us. Let go, let God. And let's get going.

March 7, 2022

STRESS THE POSITIVE

No human being ever had to endure greater hardship than Jesus, and He never lost His trust in the Father, nor His positive attitude.

During my adult life I think I've been pretty successful with helping people keep a positive attitude. Whether it was a work colleague struggling with a career challenge or a friend in the midst of a difficult time, I stressed the positive, saying simple things like, "You're not going to make it any better by worrying about it" or "just have a positive attitude – more times than not, it's mind over matter."

I've tried to follow this advice in my own life. When successful I feel better, and things generally work out in a good way. Unfortunately, I'm not always so good at following my own advice. Sometimes an upcoming event will get me worrying and I can't shake off the feeling. I tell myself the same advice that I give others. It usually works for a bit, but then I'm right back at it. The anxiety is not helpful – it does me no good at all, and it never changes the situation I'm worried about.

But it doesn't stop there. There's a knock-on effect in my relationship with God. I spend so much time consumed in worry that I actually spend less time with God. Moreover, the time I that I do spend with God is not as meaningful because I'm pre-occupied. And then I start to worry about my relationship with God. It becomes an absolute mess – a vicious circle. Ironically, the underlying cause – what I'm worrying about – frequently is a trivial matter if I were to step back and put things in the proper context.

How do I fix this problem? The first step is pretty simple: I need to acknowledge that my negative attitude isn't helping the situation. It's not helping me. It's not helping those around me. And it's hurting my relationship with Jesus. The second step is easy as well: I need to turn to Jesus. He is our constant companion who stands ready to offer both comfort and guidance. If we stop to think about it, there's no one who is in a better position to provide these gifts to someone who is worried. No human being ever had to endure greater hardship than Jesus, and He never lost His trust in the Father, nor His positive attitude.

In her book *Jesus Always*, Sarah Young provides some very good advice: "Stop your incessant worry-planning! Draw your mind back from the future to the present moment, where My presence lovingly awaits you." (*Jesus Always*, p. 83; Thomas Nelson). We all have a tendency to obsess over the issues we're about to face: especially a challenging meeting, a doctor's appointment or a tough discussion with a family member. Jesus tells us to bring our minds back to the present, to live in the moment with Him.

If we live in the present with Him, Jesus will help to change our channel and refocus on the positive. Sarah Young also writes, "When problems are weighing heavily on you, your natural tendency is to speed up your pace of living, frantically searching for answers. But what you need at such times is to *slow down* and seek My face." (*Jesus Always*, p. 84).

We, or at least I, spend too much time in our daily lives overcomplicating things, constantly trying to solve problems (sometimes before they even become problems!). And when we do that, we can actually slow down progress. Instead, Jesus preaches patience, quiet time with Him and trust in Him. In fact, He stresses the opposite of complications. His solution is overly simple: "Seek my face."

While it may be simple, it's not always easy. However, if we can slow down and live in the present – if we can earnestly seek His face – we will in fact change our channel. We will stress the positive no matter the current or future situation in our lives. The issues we're facing may not go away, but our reaction to them will change. We – with God's help, and that's the key – will control the problem instead of it controlling us. Jesus never abandons us. Let's always stress the positive by turning to Jesus.

September 22, 2023

PAUL E. TUPPER

BEING CLOSE TO JESUS

It typically doesn't take a lot of effort to be close to Jesus. It certainly isn't difficult. However, it does require a small investment of time ⁻ time to be with Jesus in prayer/thought or time spent with others doing God's will.

The invitation to have a close personal relationship with Jesus is open to all of us – every single person. Jesus doesn't discriminate. Granted, it is probably easier for those who take time to be with Jesus every day, but the invitation is available to all, as is the path to Heaven.

If we stop to think about it, it's not hard to become close to Jesus. He made it so simple for us. By dying on the cross, Jesus broke the barrier of sin that separated us from Him and His Father. By rising, He opened the gates of Heaven for us. Finally, by coming to us and living within us in the form of the Holy Spirit, He is available to us all the time. It's not necessary to go to a church or anywhere else to spend time with Jesus. He's already with us, just waiting for us to acknowledge Him and be with Him.

I'm one who tends to over-complicate just about everything. More than once, I've had to remind myself that this is not about having some profound theological conversation with Jesus or memorizing Scripture and reciting it back to Him. No. Although we certainly can find Jesus through those actions, we can develop a closer friendship with Him through very simple acts: For example, talking to Jesus while taking a walk (talking to Him about anything). This is one of the most effective ways I find closeness with Jesus. Sometimes it's just saying, "Thank you, God" or "I trust in You, Jesus." In short, it's reminding ourselves that Jesus is present in everyday moments and in everyday conversations.

We can also feel close to Jesus when we do small acts of kindness for others, whether we know them or not: For example, letting someone go ahead of us in line at the grocery store, saying thank you, spending time to listen to someone who needs to get something off their chest or offering a hand to someone who is having difficulty carrying their bags.

Just a few hours ago I was leaving the local bakery with a bag full of goodies to bring to my mother-in-law when I visit her later today. I spotted an elderly man using a walker who had just gotten up from his table in front of the bakery. He was moving toward his car, pushing the walker and holding a cup of coffee. I started to walk away, back toward my house. Then I realized that maybe he might need assistance. I walked back to him and asked if I could help. He looked at me and said he was fine. I noticed he was wearing a New York Giants cap – my favorite football team. I commented that I hoped the Giants would play better next season. He laughed and we talked sports for a few minutes. He then thanked me and we parted ways. I didn't do anything to actually help him, but I think he appreciated the offer. Hopefully, that encounter was pleasant for him. It certainly was for me. It may sound silly, but I felt closer to Jesus after that moment.

It typically doesn't take a lot of effort to be close to Jesus. It certainly isn't difficult. However, it does require a small investment of time – time to be with Jesus in prayer/thought or time spent with others doing God's will. And like most relationships, the more time we put into it, the closer our relationship with Jesus will become.

This offer of a close personal relationship with Jesus is given to all of us freely. There is nothing any of us did to deserve this incredible blessing. May we remember to be thankful for this gift from God, and may we demonstrate our thankfulness by accepting His offer and developing this precious relationship. It will be the most rewarding relationship we will ever have.

July 28, 2021

APP UPDATES

Reading and reflecting on the Scriptures is an easy way to update our spiritual lives. It requires only a few minutes each day, but in that brief time we're allowing God to influence our hearts and minds with His Word.

Incessantly we receive notifications that we should update the applications on our devices: the app for our mobile banking, the app for our favorite streaming service, the app for the rideshare service and on and on. Recently I got so annoyed at the incessant reminders that I turned off the notifications. But still that little red number count on the App Store icon is a constant reminder of how many are in need of an update. Today my count stood at 30.

It makes you wonder: how can these companies be so inefficient? The providers tell us that in some cases there is a bug or vulnerability that needs fixing; but more often they assert that most of the updates are for improvements to make our experience as users better. To be honest, I'm skeptical, but then again, as an auditor, I was trained to be "professionally skeptical." Regardless of the reason, it seems the updates are necessary for our devices to work at maximum efficiency.

Come to think of it, a similar logic applies with most aspects of our lives. Sometimes we're in need of an update.

Perhaps we feel that we've become stuck at work. The solution might be to take a training course to learn new skills. That's our app update. Or maybe we've lost the motivation to go to the gym. The same old workout routine just isn't inspiring any more. The solution could be to add some new elements to the workout or start a new routine entirely. That's the app update for us.

It's no different with our spiritual lives. If we're not consistently looking to improve, we run the risk of becoming stagnant in our faith or, worse yet, drifting away from it. Fortunately we have several "app updates" to aid us.

Reading and reflecting on the Scriptures is an easy way to update our spiritual lives. It requires only a few minutes each day, but in that brief time we're allowing God to influence our hearts and minds with His Word. It couldn't be any simpler. The only requirement is a Bible. Actually, there are even apps for that! The App Store has several biblical and other spiritual apps that can be downloaded to the phone. Just be aware: They likely will require periodic updates too!

Sometimes a vulnerability embeds itself in us – a sort of spiritual malware. Satan has taken advantage of a small opening. It's critical that we eradicate that vulnerability before it spreads within us and causes significant damage to our faith. We need an app update to destroy the malware. To get that update we should turn to Scripture. We should turn to the Word. Satan's malware is powerless against the Word.

There will be other times when our faith journey is not in need of critical care, but it can use a bit of a tune-up. We may feel like we're going through the motions when we pray. We need an update. The Word of God – the Word made flesh – is our update.

The amazing thing is that we can have these updates whenever we need them. Unlike the updates on our phones where the provider pushes them to us, we have total control over our spiritual updates. We can get as many as we want whenever we want them. Why? Because these updates are facilitated by the Holy Spirit, and the Holy Spirit dwells within us.

There's a small catch, however. These updates require action steps on our part. First, we have to request them. We must ask the Holy Spirit to refresh our souls. Then we must invest the time to let Him do that. We need to spend time reading Scripture and praying to God. In the end our investment will be well worth it. God's updates will protect our souls from malware threats and recharge our spiritual lives. His Word will continuously renew our faith.

March 18, 2024

PUT IT ON THE HOUSE ACCOUNT

We didn't earn our inheritance into everlasting life; God freely gave it to us through the sacrifice of His Son.

There's a nice clothing store that I like to shop at. They let me establish a house account there so I can charge things automatically. It's a neat feeling to shop, find some things that I like, approach the check-out person and say, "Put it on the house account." Because I'm not putting the charge on my credit card or paying cash, I have a brief feeling that I didn't have to pay for it... Well, at least until the bill comes in the mail a few weeks later.

It occurred to me that our religious experience is somewhat like a house account. When He suffered, died and rose, Jesus essentially set up a house account for each of us. He saved us from our sins and secured for us a place in Heaven. I was reading a Bible commentary today and the reflection was on the following passage, perhaps the most recognized verse in the Gospels: "For God so loved the world that He gave His only Son, so that everyone who believes in Him should not perish but have everlasting life." (Jn3:16).

We didn't earn our inheritance into everlasting life; God freely gave it to us through the sacrifice of His Son. And unlike the house account at my favorite store, we won't receive a bill. We get the greatest gifts of all – forgiveness for our sins, an invitation to have a personal relationship with Jesus and an inheritance of eternal life—and they're free. All that's required is we believe in Him and be thankful. That's one amazing house account!

July 6, 2022

PAUL E. TUPPER

OUR EASTER GIFT

After His Resurrection and Ascension, Jesus returned to us through the Holy Spirit and dwells within each of us today so He can show us the way to those gates, just as He led Jean. That's our Easter gift.

Today is Easter Sunday, a celebration of one of the most remarkable events in all human history and, fittingly, the most glorious feast in the church year. As I reflected on this special day, my thoughts centered around two basis messages.

First, Christ died for us. He didn't just give His life to save those who had gone before Him or for His contemporaries. He also suffered, died and rose for each of us, so that we can go to Heaven and be with Him.

This message became very personal for me on Easter Sunday two years ago. It was my first Easter without Jean, my late wife. She had passed away six months earlier after battling cancer. Jean and I always attended mass together, and the Easter mass was particularly special for her. Easter Sunday two years ago occurred in the early stages of the Covid pandemic, so the churches were closed. I watched the mass on television.

During the celebration, I had an epiphany that absolutely overwhelmed me. I suddenly realized that because Jesus died and rose, Jean was in Heaven! This was a direct "cause-and-effect" event – Jesus' death and resurrection led to Jean's resurrection in Heaven. When she died, I believed that Jean went to Heaven. But on that Easter Sunday, I became absolutely sure in my heart that Jean is in Heaven, thanks to Jesus' mercy. There was simply no doubt in my mind.

This realization was astonishing. It was a good thing that I was sitting in my living room and not in the church because I became extremely emotional, probably the most emotional I've ever been. I cried tears of joy and screamed and started to pump my fists in the air as if my sports team had just won the championship. And, in fact, that's a good analogy. Because of what Jesus did, He won the contest, and the prize for Jean and all of us who believe is Heaven.

Jesus died and rose – for Jean and for all of us. That must be why people in Heaven are so happy: they've realized that they are there because of what Jesus did. On that Easter Sunday in 2020, the Resurrection became very personal for me because it had a direct effect on my wife. Hopefully, someday it will for me also.

The second message is related: The Resurrection, although it is a historical event, is a present tense word. Jesus *is* risen! For most of my adult life, I had not focused on this fact; my mindset was that Jesus died and rose and saved us from our sins. That's true, but there's more. Jesus dwells within us today – each one of us. He's there whenever we remember to call on Him. We may notice it more when we're in trouble and call out to Him. But He's with us all the time and wants us to talk to Him, to share our joys with Him, to share our sorrows, and yes, our grief, to ask for His mercy or simply ask for companionship. Whatever our situation, He's there if we just turn to Him.

His living presence within us is possible because of the Resurrection and the Ascension. Those two events made it possible for Jesus to come to each of us today through His Holy Spirit. Even the Apostles couldn't all turn to Him for help at the same time while Jesus lived among them. Jesus had to die, rise, and ascend to Heaven, so God could send the Holy Spirit to dwell within each of them then and each of us now.

The Resurrection is personal. Yes, Jesus died and rose for our ancestors, for our relatives, for Jean. But He also died and rose for us – to free us from sin and open the gates of Heaven. After His Resurrection and Ascension, Jesus returned to us through the Holy Spirit and dwells within each of us today so He can show us the way to those gates, just as He led Jean. That's our Easter gift. It's no wonder we are so joyful on this day.

April 18, 2022

EASTER PEOPLE

What matters is that we are present ⁻ at Easter Sunday mass. We're there to honor the Risen Lord and to sing praises because He died for our sins and rose from the dead to show us the way to Heaven.

Easter Sunday – the holiest, most solemn feast day of the entire church year. We all have our traditions: Easter egg hunts, a delicious Easter omelet, baked ham with all the trimmings and, of course, Easter cookies. Rumor has it my sister saved me some of her famous Easter cookies for my visit next weekend. I hope the rumor is true!

One tradition that almost all of us have in common is attending Easter Sunday mass. The church is filled – standing room only – and the attendees are dressed in their best spring outfits. This year was no exception. My son and I attended mass near our house in Florida. We arrived early but the church was already full, so we stood along the side aisle. As we waited for mass to start, I took in the scene. The altar was filled with beautiful flowers, and there were white bows on the end of each pew. There was a choir and a horn section, and they combined with the pipe organ to create amazing music. I observed as people flowed into the church. Not surprisingly, most were dressed to the nines – flowing dresses, nice suits, colorful ties, fancy shoes and even snappy hats. It seemed no detail was missed. What a fitting way to honor the Risen Lord!

As I stood there, I asked myself why it wasn't like this every weekend. After all, at each mass we commemorate Jesus' death and resurrection and receive His body. Why do so many people attend services only on Easter and Christmas? I put the thought out of my head, though, realizing that my focus should be on Jesus.

What matters is that we are present – at Easter Sunday mass. We're there to honor the Risen Lord and to sing praises because He died for our sins and rose from the dead to show us the way to Heaven. It's the most glorious of days, so it's fitting that the church is filled to the rafters and that everyone is dressed up. There was a different feel to the mass because of this. I couldn't help but think that Jesus was smiling as He looked down upon from Heaven – at us and all the people attending Mass on this special day. We had come to honor our Lord and Savior!

On that first Easter Sunday two-thousand years ago, Mary Magdalene arrived at the tomb early in the morning. When she realized that the body of Jesus was gone, she was despondent. "Where have you taken him?," she asked a man who she thought was the gardener. In response, Jesus revealed Himself to her. (John 20:15-16). Mary rejoiced upon seeing Jesus alive. In a moment, her grief had turned to joy.

Just imagine the depth of Mary's emotions. Three days prior, she had watched in horror as Jesus was tortured and then crucified. Her Savior who had miraculously healed her was gone. To compound her misery, she came to the tomb only to find His body gone. Her world was spiraling out of control.

And then, in a moment, everything changed. She saw the Risen Lord, the one who had forgiven her sins – the one who forgives our sins. He was raised, and there were no more tears. Mary was overjoyed and ran to tell the Apostles. Mary was the first to witness Jesus' resurrection – she was the first Easter person.

On Easter Sunday, we go to find Jesus too. Unlike Mary, however, we already know the ending to this glorious story. We won't find Jesus in the tomb. We know Jesus is Risen and that He dwells among us, or rather, within us. And, like Mary, we are overjoyed. On Easter Sunday we dress in our finest outfits and go to meet Jesus and rejoice with Him. Like Mary, we are Easter people.

He is Risen, and that changes everything.

April 9, 2024

BEING THANKFUL

Instead of asking Him "Why me?", we can say, "God, thank you for always being close to me. Please help me to get through this challenge I'm facing." This subtle but profound shift in attitude can be a game-changer...

Lately there has been a theme running through the spiritual books I'm reading – being thankful. The gist is that it's easy to be grateful when things are going well. However most of us struggle to have an attitude of thankfulness when we're facing challenges. Ironically, it's precisely during such difficult times that we must focus on being thankful.

I vividly remember the day I made partner at my public accounting firm. I was working on a project out of town in Atlanta. Late in the afternoon I received a call from a senior partner in the Firm telling me the good news. Having worked toward this goal for most of my career and to have finally achieved it – I was ecstatic. After work I returned to my hotel room, sat down, closed my eyes and thanked God for His blessings. It was because of His grace that I achieved this career milestone. I sat there for a long while, not saying much of anything other than offering thanks. I can remember it as if it were yesterday.

That day was a highlight in my career. There have been other moments that clearly were not highlights. One stands out – a very time-sensitive client project in Mexico City. Our team had been working long, stressful days. One night I got back to my hotel room at about 11 p.m. We had completed the assignment, or so I thought. I was exhausted and started to nod off. Then the phone rang. It was the lead partner calling from New York. He informed me that the client added another element to the project and it absolutely had to be finished by the morning. Reluctantly I trudged back to the office and worked through the night to complete it. I was frustrated and found myself asking God, "Why is this happening to me?"

Looking back on it, that assignment was a small bump in the road of a long career, but at the time I felt like the world was caving in on me. With a slight change in my perspective I think I would have completed the project with much less stress. The work was going to get done either way. What if, instead of complaining to God, I thanked Him that I had a job at all and one that I enjoyed? What if I had spent a minute praising Him for the fact that, due to His grace, I was able to provide for my family?

Being thankful keeps us connected to God. In my case, when I feel connected to Him, I worry less about things. When we're connected it's easier to remember to ask Jesus for help. Instead of asking Him "Why me?", we can say, "God, thank you for always being close to me. Please help me to get through this challenge I'm facing." This subtle but profound shift in attitude can be a game-changer in terms of reducing stress. It's much easier be relaxed when you are thankful.

Jesus expressed His gratitude to the Father throughout the Gospels. In the Gospel of Matthew, He says "Father… I offer you praise; for what you have hidden from the learned and clever, you have revealed to the merest children." (Matthew 11:25). The Lord's prayer starts with a verse of praise ("hallowed be thy name"). And, most significantly, what does Jesus do at the Last Supper before He breaks the bread? He gives thanks to His Father. In Luke it is written, "Then, taking bread and giving thanks, he broke it and gave it to them…" (Luke 22:19). Think about it for a minute. Jesus, knowing full well what He was about to endure, thanked His Father. He was about to suffer in a way that none of us ever will experience, and He thanked God. And what was the result of the suffering that Jesus endured? Victory over death – forever. Jesus was able to see the end game and that made Him thankful. We too know the end game, and we similarly should always be thankful.

March 11, 2023

JOY IN FINDING JESUS

When I stop to reflect on it, spending time to learn about Jesus is a win/win. I'm doing something that I really like (I've always liked reading and learning), and I'm doing the will of God by learning more about Him.

It's the fruit of the last Joyful Mystery of the Holy Rosary: joy in finding Jesus. We reflect on this mystery twice each week when we recite the Rosary. What a fitting way to end the Joyful Mysteries -- with a reference to finding Jesus, and the joy that emanates from that encounter.

A few years ago, I had a deeply spiritual experience while attending Mass at my favorite church in New York City. I had arrived early to say the Rosary before Mass. It was the Saturday vigil Mass, so I was reciting the Joyful Mysteries. As I started on the fifth Mystery – "Finding the Child Jesus in the Temple" — I felt something stir inside me. I've recited this mystery many times, but today it dawned on me: There absolutely is joy in finding Jesus.

Over the months leading up to that experience, I had been in the process of finding Jesus through prayers, quiet refection, Scripture reading and the like. I discovered that the more I learned about Jesus and His love, the more I wanted to know – perhaps like the people in the temple listening to the child Jesus preach. And as I continue even today to "find" Jesus, the joy I feel increases – perhaps just like the joy His parents felt on that day they found Him in the temple.

As I prayed that fifth decade, Jesus spoke to me: "Keep reading Scripture and other religious books. Do it more!" Jesus did not speak the words in a tone that was chiding me, but rather in the vein of encouragement. He knew that I was really enjoying learning more about Him and developing my faith, and He wanted me to continue. Although Jesus didn't say it directly, the words that came into my mind were, "Become a student of me." When I stop to reflect on it, spending time to learn about Jesus is a win/win. I'm doing something that I really like (I've always liked reading and learning), and I'm doing the will of God by learning more about Him.

The exclamation point to this encounter came about 30 minutes later, during Mass. It was the feast day of St. Ignatius of Loyola. During the homily the priest provided some context on the conversion of Ignatius. He described how Ignatius always had an appetite for reading adventure stories (e.g., knights in shining armor). One day Ignatius was being treated for a serious injury sustained in battle, and he asked for some of these adventure books. The hospital didn't have any, and instead gave him what they had: a book on the life of Jesus and several books on the saints. Ignatius started to read. As he did, Ignatius realized that he wanted to learn more, and so he kept reading. Ultimately, he discovered that the books on Christ and the saints satisfied him both temporally and spiritually. The more he read about them, the more he wanted to know. Moreover, Ignatius experienced peace when he was reading the books. Not surprisingly, this experience started his conversion. It's also no surprise that the religious order Ignatius founded, the Society of Jesus, or Jesuits, are known for their scholarly pursuits.

As is so often the case with our encounters with Jesus, the two events I experienced in the New York church were not a coincidence. There is no doubt in my mind that Jesus combined them to more strongly convey His will and ministry for me. I can be oblivious at times, but this one was hard to miss. And, as is so often the case, Jesus works through our strengths – reading and learning is something that I like to do. In the end, Jesus is preparing each of us for the ministry He wants us to carry out.

Jesus will communicate His will for us if we allow Him into our lives. If we acknowledge that His Holy Spirit dwells within us, if we let the Spirit speak to us and direct our thoughts, if we respond to His promptings, if we're patient, Jesus will guide us toward the ministry He has planned for each of us. And, we will experience joy in finding Jesus.

October 25, 2023

MY EMMAUS

He wants us to be closer to Him, and He wants to help us succeed in our efforts to do so. Only God, who's love for us is so strong, would want to help us love Him too.

Today's Gospel reading described the experience of two disciples who met Jesus on their way to Emmaus after His death and resurrection. They spent hours in conversation with Him, but they didn't realize who He was until He broke bread with them later at dinner. It's one of my favorite Gospel passages – I can quite easily put myself in the scene and then imagine Jesus coming along and recounting Scripture. I love their statement, "Were not our hearts burning within us..." I can almost feel what they must have been experiencing. They knew something special was happening even if they didn't realize at the time that Jesus was with them. Who wouldn't be touched in a personal way if Jesus were walking among them and speaking to them?

The truth is we can each have our own Emmaus experience every day. Because Jesus dwells within us, we are able to experience His presence in a very personal way. Jesus doesn't require much from us to experience Him. We merely need to put aside the distractions of life for a few moments and seek Him, call to Him. Maybe the disciples in the Gospel story can serve as an example to us. They encountered Jesus when they were walking along on the road – alone, away from the city (of Jerusalem) with all of its distractions. When they were quiet and focused, Jesus appeared. It can be the same for us. But too often with me such a simple act is difficult. Even when I have the best of intentions, I often don't find the inner peace that enables me to connect personally with Jesus.

In my own situation, I think there are three things that I can do to increase the likelihood of having that personal encounter with Jesus: Be more patient when I am trying to create quiet time to connect with Him (too often I give up quickly); be more persistent (keep at it every day, even when I don't get the results I'm hoping for); and, maybe most importantly, ask the Holy Spirit to help.

Quite often I think we forget the most obvious solution. In my case, I'm too quick to think it's circular: How can I ask God for help in becoming closer to Him?? Yet that's exactly what He wants us to do. He wants us to be closer to Him, and He wants to help us succeed in our efforts to do so. Only God, who's love for us is so strong, would want to help us love Him too.

Speaking from personal experience it is most definitely worth the effort. There have been times – admittedly, not as frequently as I would like – where I feel so close to Jesus that I actually experience the joy in my heart. At those times, I think I have an idea of what those disciples experienced on the road to Emmaus.

April 20, 2022

A THANK YOU PRAYER

Jesus, thank you for humbling yourself to become like us and live among us.

Thank you for teaching us and showing us the way to the Father.

Thank you for giving your life so that we could live.

Thank you for rising and ascending to Heaven, so that Heaven would be open to us.

Thank you for coming to live within each of us every day through your Holy Spirit.

Thank you for giving me my faith in you.

Thank you for your unwavering faith in me even when my faith in you wavers.

Thank you for your steadfast faith in me, even when I don't have faith in myself.

Thank you for your mercy – for always being willing to forgive my sins.

Thank you for being there for me during the difficult times.

Thank you for being the One I can <u>always</u> count on. Even when those closest to me let me down, you never do.

Thank you for never letting me down even when I let you down.

Thank you for bringing such special people into my life – people who serve as a daily reminder of how I can live a Christian life.

Thank you for bringing joy into my life and for rejoicing in my happiness.

Thank you for your guidance – helping me to understand how to live as you want me to.

Thank you for your patience in me when I don't have any in myself.

Thank you for wanting to have a personal relationship with me, even though I don't deserve it.

Thank you for never giving up on me.

Thank you for being my Savior.

April 27, 2022

FEELING SPECIAL

...God makes us feel special every moment that we put ourselves in His presence.

Have you ever had one of those experiences that you know you'll remember for years to come? Have you ever been treated like royalty? Yesterday was one of those times for me.

Jessica and I were invited as special guests to a grand reopening of a retail store in New York that I occasionally shop at. The hosts pulled out all the stops to make sure their guests were treated in a special way. We had a champagne cocktail and an exquisite brunch, followed by a private tour of the magnificently refurbished building. We were even given a huge bag filled with parting gifts. It was a spectacular day, made even more special by the fact that I was able to share it with my better half. I think she enjoyed it also! There was no detail that the hosts missed.

As the day was winding down, there was one more thing we needed to do. It was a Sunday, and because we had been at the event all day, we had not gone to Mass yet. Fortunately, we were near St. Patrick's Cathedral and they had a late Sunday afternoon service. We braved the pouring rain and made it in time for Mass.

As amazing as our day at the retailer had been, the Mass

was even more special. The church was beautifully decorated with flowers throughout, reflecting the Easter season, and the pipe organ generated rhythmic sounds. More importantly, it was peaceful. In an instant, we went from the lights and glitter of the opening event, the hustle and bustle of the city streets to the peace of God's house. And isn't that how it always is? We always find an inner peace when we put ourselves in the presence of God.

As if to add an exclamation point on this special afternoon, I realized it was Good Shepherd Sunday. The image of Jesus as the Good Shepherd has always been one of my favorites. In my Catholic school days, the nuns had us memorize the words of Psalm 23. I can still recite most of it from memory some 40 years later. The poetic words are so calming. Similarly, Jesus' words in the Gospel are calming for us. In His own words, He is the Good Shepherd who lays down His life for His sheep (John 10:11) – for us. For a shepherd, it was second nature to risk his life for his flock. He would do anything to protect them from harm. That's exactly what Jesus did for us. He gave up His life for us. Moreover, He sent His Holy Spirit to dwell within us and help us when we encounter difficulties. Just as the sheep find peace because of the shepherd, we can find peace because of our Good Shepherd. There definitely is no detail that God misses in His care of us.

During our lives, we may feel special for moments here and there like I did yesterday, and it's no doubt a great feeling. But God makes us feel special every moment that we put ourselves in His presence. We may be made to feel like royalty on occasion here on earth. But in fact, we <u>are</u> royalty in God's eyes. We're so important to Him that He sent us His Son to redeem us.

No matter what is going on in our lives, we can find peace with God. When we're stressed about something, we can turn to God, and He will comfort and reassure us. When we're on an emotional high we can turn to Him, and He will rejoice in our happiness. Moreover, being with God will amplify our happiness. In my case yesterday, sitting in St. Patrick's reminded me that, while we have those transitory perfect moments like I did at the event, with God we're on the path toward an eternity of perfect moments. Jesus truly is our Good Shepherd, and that should make us feel special – like royalty.

May 1, 2023

SEEK HIS FACE

My mind took me to a place that was bright and peaceful. I could sense light although my eyes were closed. For a short period of time, all the craziness of life receded. I felt the presence of Jesus.

It seems we're always waiting for life to slow down. We never seem to have enough time. Life is getting more complicated every day. How often have we heard these statements or maybe even uttered them ourselves? I know I have – quite frequently.

At work I was seldom able to get through my daily "to do" list. Fairly often my solution was to work late into the evening. Of course, that took time away from my family and other personal responsibilities. Which, in turn, made me frustrated. It can easily become a vicious circle. When I was in a particularly busy stretch with one of my clients, I often would say to myself: "I just need to get through this phase. Then things will slow down, and I can take a breath." Not surprisingly, that seldom happened.

That's just the way life is today. Even now, although I'm retired, life still seems to be relentlessly busy. It may ebb and flow from day to day, but we all know by now that we shouldn't expect life to slow down and become easy.

Jesus gives us an answer to this problem: Seek His face. In the midst of our busy lives, Jesus urges us to carve out some time for Him. He doesn't demand much – in fact, almost nothing. He merely wants us to take some time each day and be in His presence. We can do that by praying, reading Scripture, meditating or by just sitting quietly and clearing our minds of all of the noise. That's when we will be able to seek His face.

I must admit – I didn't really know exactly what that phrase meant. I still may not know for sure. But I can say that, after hearing someone say "seek His face" recently, I sat down and tried. I blocked out everything else and searched for the face of Jesus in my mind. In response, I can't say that a clear image of Him appeared. However, I certainly did experience Jesus in a special way. My mind took me to a place that was bright and peaceful. I could sense light although my eyes were closed. For a short period of time, all the craziness of life receded. I felt the presence of Jesus. I was able to focus -- if just for a little while – on what's really important.

It's simple, but it's remarkable. In our busy lives where things never seem to slow down, we too easily forget the obvious. While we may not be able to control what happens in our lives, we <u>can</u> put ourselves in the hands of Jesus and give Him control. All it takes is a little bit of quiet time and the willingness to defer to Him. When we do, things don't seem as crazy. Life even slows down a bit. Everything we then do is considered in the broader context of why we are here on this earth. And we will have more energy to face our daily tasks and trials because we can always look to Jesus and feel Him right there by our side. In sum, we can create a virtuous circle with Jesus.

When we seek His face, we find His presence.

March 2, 2023

THE PROPER PERSPECTIVE

*Pray, hope and don't worry. Worry is useless.
God is merciful and will hear your prayer.*

─ *Simple but sage wisdom from
a great saint, Padre Pio.*

When we read these words, they instantly make sense to us. Why would we ever worry about anything? We know God hears our prayers and will help us.

Yet, as with so many things in our lives, what makes sense in theory can be very hard to put into practice. At least this is true for me.

At work, I constantly worried. The vast majority of issues I worried about fell into two categories: matters that I couldn't do anything about because they were out of my hands (e.g., wondering how the client was going to react when I told them their proposed transaction didn't meet the accounting rules), or items that were almost certain to successfully occur (e.g., there was no doubt we would meet the client deadline even if there might be a few bumps getting there). Yet, I would be anxious. With the benefit of hindsight, it seems pretty silly now, but worry I did.

I thought the anxiety would abate upon my retirement.

Much to my chagrin, it has not. And once again, most of the things that concern me are not important in the grand scheme of things. Some are, like the safety of my son as he starts school in a new city or the health of my loved ones. But as with the previous matters at work, there is nothing I can do about these concerns.

Well, actually there is. I can follow Padre Pio's advice. I can pray, hope and leave the worrying to God. This is where it should be simple, but it's quite difficult – at least for me.

When a problem arose at work, the first thing we did was determine the root cause. Even the most complex problems are easier to solve if one can determine what provoked them. The procedure was simple: Figure out the root cause, design a solution to address it, and the problem is resolved.

I decided to figure out the root cause of my problem of worrying too much. It didn't take long to find the source. I can't let go of things. When a concern arises, I grab onto it and don't let go. I make everything important. If I don't let go, I can't leave the worrying to God. Sometimes I realize what I'm doing and am temporarily successful in turning things over to Him. But after a period of time – sometimes brief, sometimes longer – I take the problem back from Him. I imagine I'm not alone in this regard.

So now that I've determined the root cause, what's the solution? It seems to me the solution is to take some time to reflect and put things into the proper perspective. Is the matter important or not? Is there an action step we can take to change the outcome?

If the matter is not important, then we shouldn't be worrying about it. Full stop.

If the matter is important and we can take an action that might impact the outcome, by all means we should take that action. Stop worrying and do it.

If the matter is important and we cannot make a direct impact by our actions, we must realize that no amount of worrying is going to change the outcome. However, God can direct the outcome. Therefore, the action we should take is to pray to Him.

There may be an even simpler solution. If we pray to God about everything, there won't be an opportunity to worry because we will already have given all our concerns over to God.

Pray, hope and don't worry. Worry is useless.
God is merciful and will hear your prayer.

August 9, 2023

MANAGING OUR SPIRITUAL LIVES

We just need to get focused and decide that our spiritual lives are important ⁻ in reality, more important than the other aspects of our lives ⁻ and then appropriately prioritize.

I spend a lot of time attempting to manage my schedule. In fact, I think I'm the king of trying to manage my time. When I was working, I managed my schedule on a micro and macro level. The funny part is that despite my efforts, the old adage generally rang true: Man plans, and God laughs.

On the micro level, I mapped out each day very tightly. Upon arriving at the office in the morning, I dutifully wrote out my "to-do" list – things I needed to accomplish that day. I looked at what meetings were already on my calendar and I attempted to carve out time to get my list done. Of course, despite my efforts, my plan for the day typically went completely awry as soon as the phone started ringing and the day's problems emerged.

On a macro level, I continuously reassessed my career: Where I was at a point in time, where I wanted to get to and how to keep improving. Even today in retirement, I'm still constantly creating "to-do" lists to help me manage being a parent, being a son, taking care of the house, being on top of the finances, etc. As I said, I spend a lot of time trying to manage my schedule!

At Mass today, the priest mentioned that we should manage our spiritual lives. That got me thinking. I must admit that I've never thought about managing my spiritual life. It's ironic because it's much more important than all the other activities I mentioned above. And it's even more interesting because, lately, I've been disappointed in myself for not doing a good job responding to God's calling. Well, attending Mass today gave me the solution.

I need to manage my spiritual life – my time with God – with the same focus that I attempt to manage everything else in my life. And I need to manage it on both a micro and macro level. First, I should ask myself: What am I doing today to make sure I achieve my spiritual goals – i.e., what does God want me to do? Then I should ask myself: How am I doing from a spiritual career perspective?

When I was working, my macro goal was to make partner, and once I had achieved that to advance and become the lead partner on larger clients. For my spiritual career, my goal is to make sure that I am fulfilling the plan that God has set out for me, and ultimately to be deemed worthy of entering Heaven when I leave this life.

You would think it would be relatively easy for me to manage my spiritual life. I've had a lot of practice in the area of managing things. After all, I'm the king of managing my schedule, or at least trying to. The reality is it's not going to be easy. But fortunately I have help. We all have help.

Just like we have people who help us manage our

activities – performance managers at work, mentors, personal financial advisers, to name a few – we have plenty of help when it comes to managing our spiritual lives: priests, spiritual advisers, sacred scripture, and most importantly, Jesus Himself. In fact, we have all the help we need. We just need to get focused and decide that our spiritual lives are important – in reality, more important than the other aspects of our lives – and then appropriately prioritize.

I have a feeling that if we do this, it's going to create a balance in our overall lives that will make everything else easier to manage, not to mention that we'll be able to approach those other areas with the proper perspective. It's really a no-brainer, isn't it?

So let's make it a priority to actively manage our spiritual lives. Better yet, let's turn our spiritual lives over to Jesus and let Him manage them.

September 28, 2022

SMALL SEEDS

We're never going to be able to eliminate all the bad seeds from our lives - we're human. However, what we can do is be vigilant and quickly identify them.

In today's Gospel, Jesus preaches a parable to the crowds, comparing the kingdom of God to a mustard seed. It is the smallest of all seeds, but grows to become the largest of all plants. (Mark 4:31-32) Among other messages, I think He is telling us that little things help to advance our faith and God's kingdom.

We have numerous examples in the Church of holy people doing little things. For example, Saint Therese of Lisieux's mantra was doing little things for others, and through those actions, serving Christ. Little things can produce big results when we do them for God. It's the ultimate virtuous circle.

Unfortunately the opposite is true, too. When we do little things that are not in accord with God's will (or don't do little things that are), we turn away from God. It's frequently just a very slight turn. It's easy to rationalize away: "It's just a small thing. I'll do better tomorrow." We may not even realize it, which might be worse. Regardless, we've turned away from God.

God understands our weaknesses, and He always stands

ready to forgive us and help us avoid making the same mistakes in the future. However, the risk is that one little act leads to another and then to another. Before long, we're in the dreaded "drift," where we've gotten off the path to God. Instead of a virtuous circle we've created a vicious circle, which too easily can gather momentum.

I'm sure we've all had experiences in our everyday lives where this gradual drift has occurred. I can think of one such experience in my life. A few years ago I had a major medical issue. I was always a healthy person but this situation was traumatic, so it was a major wake-up call for me. Following the doctor's orders, I commenced a much healthier diet. I resolved to cut out all trans-fat from my meals – that meant no more fried food – no small task for me, as I loved hamburgers and French fries! I further committed myself to eating more vegetables and fruit.

I got off to a good start and even found foods that didn't make me miss my old favorites, at least for a time. I probably stayed true to the new diet for almost a year. Then I allowed myself a "cheat day" here and there. My rationalization was, "I'm doing really good. It's ok to relax today." A cheat day once in a while is fine, but unfortunately, mine became more frequent. Eventually, my cheat days started to be the norm, and I had regressed back to my previous diet. For the longest time, I didn't even realize it. And this was after a life-threatening health issue.

It's the same with our spiritual lives. We have the best of intentions, and we really want to follow God's will and plan for us. We pray every day. We attend Mass regularly. We pray the Rosary regularly. We strive to respond to the needs of others.

Inevitably, there is an interruption. Life happens. We have a long day at work and by the time we get home we just want to go to bed. "I'm too exhausted to say my evening prayers. I'll skip them tonight and get back to it tomorrow night." Or, "I didn't sleep well last night. I don't have the energy to get up and go to Mass today. I'll say a prayer instead and go tomorrow." Finally, "I have too much to do today. I don't have time to call my aunt who is by herself and has no one to talk to her. She'll understand."

These little actions too are small seeds, but not good seeds. However, like good seeds, they also grow if we don't consciously eradicate them. If left unaddressed, they eventually can choke out the good seeds in us. Hence the vicious circle.

We're never going to be able to eliminate all the bad seeds from our lives – we're human. However, what we can do is be vigilant and quickly identify them. Awareness of these undesirable small incidents and a conscious effort to not repeat them will relegate them as isolated actions.

Also, it's important to remind ourselves of the small but good things we do and how they make us feel. That will keep our focus on the positive rather than the negative. Finally, let's remember to continuously thank God for all the gifts He has given us and keep our minds focused on doing things that are pleasing to Him to show our appreciation. Small seeds can create a virtuous circle.

January 27, 2023

IT'S NOT A CHECK-THE-BOX EXERCISE

Just like with our careers, if we want our faith to grow, we must go beyond the minimum requirements. We need to understand the bigger picture. What is the bigger picture? We are children of God, and we have been saved because of His love.

For most of us, life consists of routines. In fact, I think that, for many of us, that's how we prefer it to be – it's helpful to have checklists to navigate through the day. In particular, we typically have a routine that we follow at work. We have our list of items we need to accomplish in any given day, and we dutifully power through them. In my case, as I knocked off an item, I would say that I've "checked the box." In other words, I completed my task.

Routines are helpful and checking items off our list is certainly good. However, I'm not sure about you, but my supervisors would not have thought very highly of my performance if I did nothing beyond clearing the items off my checklist day after day. Similarly, I expected more from those working for me as I started to lead teams. The best performers did all the tasks they were assigned and did them well. In addition, they looked beyond their immediate responsibilities. They strived to understand the bigger picture and worked hard to help ensure that we, as a team, were progressing toward our goals. They looked out for colleagues who may have been struggling with their responsibilities and provided assistance. Instead of merely checking the box, they thought outside the box. They did more. Invariably, these individuals were the most valuable members on our team.

How does this analogy translate into our spiritual lives and responsibilities? Unfortunately for many of us, our Christian lives can easily become a check-the-box exercise. We know that we're supposed to go to Mass every Sunday, that we should put money in the collection basket, and that it's good to pray regularly. We might be tempted to think that's enough to fulfill our Christian responsibilities. It's not.

We know that our Christian responsibilities extend beyond these actions. However, with our lives being so busy, it's easy to fall into the trap of thinking that checking the box is enough. Certainly during very busy times in our lives, the minimum may be all that we can do, and God understands that. It definitely happens to me. However, if we're being honest with ourselves, those crazy times – when we can't do anything beyond attending Mass – occur infrequently.

Just like with our careers, if we want our faith to grow, we must go beyond the minimum requirements. We need to understand the bigger picture. What is the bigger picture? We are children of God, and we have been saved because of His love. "God so loved the world that he gave his only Son that whoever believes in him may not die but may have eternal life." (John 3:16) It's one of the most quoted of all Scripture passages and for good reason.

When we realize what Jesus did for us – that His death and resurrection give us eternal life – we should want to go above and beyond in our service for God, to thank Him for His unfathomable love. Yes, we should attend Mass on Sunday and pray regularly, but there's so much more we can do. We can look around us and see those who are struggling, whether it's with their faith or other matters in their lives. We can offer to help. Sometimes we may only need to spend a few minutes in conversation with them to make a difference. We can join a charitable organization that helps the poor. We can offer to bring faith to others by becoming active in our Church or speaking to our friends about Jesus. We can spend quiet time alone with God, and let His peace take over our lives for a bit.

Jesus' mission while He was on the earth was to preach repentance and start the Church. However, Jesus, in His daily life, went far beyond these initiatives. He continually responded to the needs of others and offered help, especially to the poor and most vulnerable. In the Gospels, we often are told that Jesus was on His way somewhere but altered His plans to respond to someone in need. He went above and beyond His basic mission.

Most of us strive to go above and beyond with our jobs. Perhaps we can follow the example of Jesus and bring the same focus to our spiritual lives.

September 7, 2023

EMBRACING THE SMALL STEPS

Jesus is patient. He knows that, for most of us, it's going to take a while to prepare ourselves to do His will. He no doubt would be happy with us even if we started with small steps.

Today is the feast day of St. Matthew. Matthew, from an outward perspective, was an unlikely Apostle. He was a tax collector, and tax collectors tended to be dishonest, often demanding more from the citizens than what was owed. Matthew was likely somewhat prosperous too, given his job. The other Apostles generally were of much simpler means. Despite his occupation, Jesus called Matthew. Although he had no doubt achieved a comfortable standard of living, Matthew left his former life behind and followed Jesus. We don't know if he dropped everything all at once or if he took some time to become Jesus' disciple, but the point is that he said yes to Jesus' call.

In my case, it's certainly taking me time to respond to Jesus. I received a calling from Jesus a few years ago and initially responded quite quickly – I retired! As I look back on it, that part was easy, although it didn't seem so at the time.

It was nice not to be going to work every day. Bu, I'm now two years into retirement, and I feel like I haven't made much progress in responding to Jesus. I'm not sure how it is for others, but for me, the process of conversion – truly saying yes to Jesus and what He wants me to do – has been challenging. It requires spending time with Him every day, and that's been part of the problem. I need to do a better job of putting aside that time each day. It's taking a while for my relationship with Jesus to mature, and just like any relationship, one must invest the time for the relationship to grow. Jesus is ready. He always is. It's up to me to hold up my end.

It's also been challenging for me to rewire. In this day and age, our jobs require us to have a fundamental level of intensity. Mine was no different, and over time intensity became a core competence for me. I didn't expect the transition of rewiring from the intensity of my former career to my new one of working for God to happen immediately. However, I really underestimated this aspect of my post-retirement life. There are still days when I'm wrapped so tightly, I'm not sure I've made any progress at all in this area.

The good news is that Jesus is patient. He knows that, for most of us, it's going to take a while to prepare ourselves to do His will. He no doubt would be happy with us even if we started with small steps.

We read in the Gospel that Matthew left everything behind and followed Jesus, implying he followed Jesus immediately. That may be true. Or it may be that it took some time for Matthew to fully leave his old life behind. We do know that Jesus, the Apostles and Matthew didn't leave town right away because we're told that Jesus ate dinner at Matthew's house that evening. So maybe Matthew's conversion was more gradual – maybe he did it in small steps. Regardless, the important point is that he said yes to Jesus and transformed his life to follow Him. We can do the same by saying yes to Jesus' calling and then taking small, simple steps to become closer to Him. Over time, those small, simple steps will add up to something bigger – a conversion to live our lives as God wants us to.

There are a few things we can do to facilitate our conversion process. First, we can focus on the positive, not the negative. Even if our spiritual progress is slow, it's progress, and we should be happy with that. Secondly, we can start by saying yes to Jesus in some small way each day, most importantly, the step of taking time to be with Jesus, whether that time is spent reading Scripture, attending Mass or in quiet mediation with Him. Perhaps, we can take a few minutes to make a phone call to a friend or relative who lives alone. That's saying yes to Jesus. Even though we may not be doing as much as we think we should, we'll soon discover that we're doing more than we did two weeks ago or a month ago. Over time, small steps can add up to big progress.

September 21, 2022

LEADING BY EXAMPLE

Our calling is to try and really understand the massive sacrifice Jesus made for us – understand it and consequently believe in it; believe in Jesus; believe that He died and rose for us, and then live our lives accordingly.

We've all heard the term "lead by example." The best supervisors I had were the ones who led by example. We all were encouraged to do the same. In fact, one of the core values at my firm was "leaders who serve." Our core values were posted throughout the offices, so we were reminded of them daily. When I became a supervisor I strove to be a leader by example. The old adage is true: if you want someone to take on a task that is challenging, there is a greater chance they will be successful if you show them that you're also willing to do it or, better yet, have done it.

Unfortunately, we too often have the opposite: leaders who feel entitled. It's not hard to see how people can develop this attitude. A person spends years working long hours to advance in their career. That person finally gets to a senior position. At that point they feel entitled and kick back, letting their subordinates do the hard work. It's time to let others make the sacrifice for a change.

As I was watching daily Mass on the computer today, I had the following thought: What God did for all of us was not what a typical person in power would do, not to mention an all-powerful being. All-powerful rulers generally don't make sacrifices for their people. They don't humble themselves before those whom they rule. They certainly don't give their own lives to save their subjects.

What God did turned conventional thinking upside down. As Tim Keller wrote, God effected the "great reversal." (*Hope in Times of Fear*, p. 71; Timothy Keller; Viking Press). God's love for us is so great that He sacrificed His only Son for us. There are certainly many other things God could have done to try and turn us away from sin. He could have taken away our free will so we wouldn't think of sinning. He could have taken the lives of everyone who sinned to create a deterrent for all others. He could have done anything – because He's God. But none of these actions would have ultimately defeated satan. The only thing that could defeat satan, the master of hate, was love. What doomed satan was the ultimate act of unconditional love – an all-powerful God freely loading all of our sins onto the shoulders of His Son who bore them and died for us. Satan can't comprehend love like this, so he can't counter it. Unconditional love conquered unconditional hate.

The minute Christ died on the Cross, satan was defeated. And he knew it. He still fights on, trying to pervert souls, and unfortunately, he still has some individual successes. He wins a battle here and there when he causes a soul to stray from God, but he already lost the war. He lost it at Calvary. Sacrificial love was victorious.

Our calling is to try and really understand the massive sacrifice Jesus made for us – understand it and consequently believe in it; believe in Jesus; believe that He died and rose for us, and then live our lives accordingly. If we do this and follow Jesus' example – love the Father, love others, be humble servants as Jesus was – we will defeat evil also. Jesus was the ultimate personification of leading by example. If we strive to follow His example, we will share in His resurrection.

March 31, 2022

OUR SPIRITUAL CHARGER

We can carve out some time each day, perhaps at the beginning and the end of the day, to be with Jesus and ask Him to give us the gift of His Holy Spirit. If we do this, we'll always be charged up and ready for whatever God may ask of us.

Recently I purchased one of those electric cars. It's kind of a novelty in that it doesn't make any noise and provides a very smooth ride. I really love the fact that I don't have to pay for gas anymore! I plug the car into an outlet in my garage at night and it's ready to go in the morning. All I'm paying for is the cost of electricity. On occasion if I'm in a rush and need a quick charge, I'll go to a supercharging station, and amazingly, the car is fully charged in 30 minutes.

While I was at Mass today, I realized that we have something very similar for our spiritual lives. Our charger is the Holy Spirit. The key difference from my car charger is that the gift of the Holy Spirit is available to us anytime, anywhere, in whatever quantity we need. Most importantly, it's free – every time.

Every one of us periodically needs recharging in our spiritual lives. We can't do it all on our own. The Apostles needed to draw strength from the Holy Spirit before they commenced their ministry to form the early Church. I'm quite certain that every one of the saints needed help. Even Jesus needed to draw strength from His Father to fulfill His plan. Before or after every significant event, the Gospels tell us that Jesus withdrew alone to pray to His Father. That was never more evident and more important than in the Garden of Gethsemane prior to His passion. He needed strength from His Father to endure His suffering and death so that He could save us.

Jesus knew He needed to turn to His Father, and He did. Often. The saints did also. I'm also fairly certain that those that I look up to in my local community – my pastor, the deacons in my church and other religious leaders – understand the need as well and turn to the Holy Spirit frequently.

My problem is I don't always realize I need to recharge spiritually. Sometimes I get so busy, so caught up in the craziness of the day, that I forget to turn to Jesus. Other times I think I can handle things on my own. I convince myself that I don't need the help. The outcome in those cases is seldom good. Finally, there are times when I'm upset and wallow in my sadness instead of turning to the Holy Spirit for strength. The outcome then is generally not good either. Just like I can't drive my car if the battery is dead, we can't expect to effectively function as good Christians if our spiritual batteries are drained.

My car doesn't charge itself. I must make the conscious decision to plug it in. Similarly, with our spiritual lives, although Jesus stands ready all the time, He's generally not going to intervene to recharge us. We must make the decision to turn to Him.

Fortunately for us, there are several options to recharge our spiritual lives. Sometimes all it takes is a few minutes of quiet time alone with Jesus. Alternatively, we can read Scripture or say a few prayers. We can kneel before the Blessed Sacrament. Finally, any time we're in need of a supercharge, all we have to do is attend Mass and receive the Holy Eucharist. There's no better way to recharge our spiritual lives than to receive Christ into our bodies through the Eucharist.

With my shiny new car, I've gotten into the habit of plugging in the charger every time I pull into my garage. In that way, it's always ready to go. What if we did the same thing with our spiritual lives? We can carve out some time each day, perhaps at the beginning and the end of the day, to be with Jesus and ask Him to give us the gift of His Holy Spirit. If we do this, we'll always be charged up and ready for whatever God may ask of us. It's easy and doesn't cost anything – just a few minutes of our time.

April 25, 2023

THE HOLY SPIRIT – OUR ENABLER

God, through His Spirit, dwells in us. It's not an abstract notion at all. In fact, it couldn't be more real or more personal.

Jesus was with the Apostles during substantially all of His public ministry. We may have a tendency to be envious of the Apostles because they spent so much time with Jesus. However, Jesus is with us too, for our entire lifetime – through the Holy Spirit. And in some ways that makes Him an even more powerful advocate for us than He was to the Apostles. Instead of walking beside us, Jesus actually dwells in us. If we turn ourselves over to Him, He will lead us, direct our thoughts, direct what we say, guide our actions and help us to avoid sin. That's more than what He was to the Apostles when He lived among them. Jesus gave the Apostles power when He lived among them, but they were still limited by their own doubts – even Peter.

However, once Jesus ascended and sent the Holy Spirit to the Apostles to dwell within them, they possessed incredible powers – witness Peter in Acts raising the woman from the dead by calling on Jesus through the Holy Spirit. Peter's faith was complete because of the Holy Spirit. That same Spirit lives within us. While most of us will not possess the powers of the Apostles, which enabled them to work wondrous miracles, there is no doubt that because of the Holy Spirit we can accomplish things we otherwise could not have done – and that itself could constitute a miracle!

If we would just turn to the Holy Spirit and ask Him to lead us and then genuinely follow, we definitely will be on a path to Heaven. This seems so simple, but it's a challenge for me. I want to turn everything over to Him, but I rarely succeed. Sometimes I do for brief periods of time, and the peace I feel is amazing. Why can't I do it all the time? The typical reasons always pop up – I get busy, life gets in the way – but they really aren't valid excuses.

If the Holy Spirit is Jesus dwelling in us, then it should be pretty easy to have a personal relationship with Jesus. I have found myself talking to Jesus more frequently during the day, and the reality is that I'm doing it through His Holy Spirit. For years I have turned to the Spirit, but in an abstract way. I've approached it in the context of the Gospel passage, "…the Spirit will guide you what to say…" For instance, before a client board meeting, I would pray "Holy Spirit, give me the wisdom to say the right thing…"

That's probably not a bad prayer (at least I was asking the Holy Spirit for help), but it doesn't even come close to harnessing the power of the Holy Spirit – the power of God. God, through His Spirit, dwells in us. It's not an abstract notion at all. In fact, it couldn't be more real or more personal. Imagine going into that board meeting knowing that God is dwelling in us! We wouldn't be afraid of anything. And that's not just the case for a meeting here or there. No, it can be every moment in our lives: every single challenge we face, if we're one with the Holy Spirit. And as noted earlier, if we're one with the Holy Spirit, by extension we're on the path to Heaven. So, as with everything with God, it's a win/win. By the way, God does most of the work.

The Holy Spirit is our enabler: He enables us to have a personal relationship with Jesus. Moreover, the Holy Spirit is our personal GPS. And like a GPS, we simply need to do three things:

1) Turn it on (say "yes" to the Spirit)

2) Trust Him

3) Follow His guidance.

If we take these simple steps, our spiritual GPS will help us to have a personal relationship with Jesus, and He will lead us to our ultimate destination!

July 23, 2021

CHRIST DWELLING IN US THROUGH THE HOLY SPIRIT

It's one of the fundamental reasons why God sent His Holy Spirit to dwell within us: to lead us back to Him.

Jesus desires to have an intimate relationship with us, and we have the ability to make that happen through the Holy Spirit. The following thought occurred to me as I was taking a walk the other day: Jesus suffered, died and rose to take away our sins and open up the gates to Heaven for us. There is no greater example of love than that. He loves us so much that He was willing to suffer brutally and die a horrific death so we can be with Him. And because God raised Him, He's with us here in the present. To emphasize – this is a <u>present tense</u> statement – Jesus is with us today! More specifically, Jesus dwells in us now. He lives within us through the Holy Spirit. So, tying the above two thoughts together, the One who committed the most merciful act of anyone in history – the One who died for us – lives within us and desires to have an intimate relationship with us. When you stop to think about it that's simply incredible.

Most people who do great things in the secular world –

the best athletes, the most successful CEOs, our political leaders – are not accessible to us. However, the One who did far more than any of them combined, the One who died to save us, the One who is God, He wants to have an intimate relationship with us. If we respond by saying yes to His invitation, we will experience happiness and peace – not a temporal peace, but Christ's peace. Also, we will be on the path to Heaven.

This notion is so powerful, but it goes against the grain of the secular world. Thus, unfortunately, many miss it. To be honest, most of the time I don't remember it. But God is patient, and He helps to nudge us forward through the Spirit. I definitely can say that, when I do remember, I invariably have a great day. I'm hoping that the combination of prayer and remembering how great the feeling is when I'm close to Jesus will help me to "lock in" to that intimate relationship more and more going forward.

To analogize, it's like practicing for a sport. The more time you spend practicing, the better you're going to get. You get out of it what you put into it. Let's put the time into developing an intimate relationship with Jesus. It's the best return on investment (of time) we'll ever have.

Here are some additional thoughts of why we all should want to have a personal relationship with Jesus through His Holy Spirit:

1) Our relationship will help us to live in the moment day by day.
   - We will have someone to turn to at any time for guidance or to share a joyous experience.
   - We will never feel alone. Jesus is always here.

We always have someone to talk to who we know is listening carefully.

- There is an inherent positive attitude that can carry us through each day. Why? The One who suffered and died to free us wants to be close to us. We can't help but feel happy when we realize this.

- We will be more aware of doing good for others and, in general, of simply being kind to others. Once again this really is inevitable. If the One we're spending time with lived His life for others, it's bound to rub off.

2) It will put us on the path to Heaven.

- This process starts off day by day, but if we really embrace it, if we practice it, the days become weeks. The weeks eventually become months, which hopefully become years. I'm certainly not at that point, but it's my goal. It's one of the fundamental reasons why God sent His Holy Spirit to dwell within us: to lead us back to Him. We can think of the Holy Spirit as our GPS to God and Heaven!

3) When our time comes to pass from this earth, our intimate friend will be the One to judge whether we are worthy of going to Heaven and attaining eternal happiness. What an auspicious time to have a judge who supports us!

July 27, 2021

PAUL E. TUPPER

THE HOLINESS OF THE EUCHARIST

The more often we receive His body and reflect on the fact that His presence in us makes us holy, the more likely it is that this condition will take root in our souls.

After some internal hemming and hawing, I decided to go to daily Mass this morning. Part of me wanted to stay in bed and start the day slowly. Fortunately the other side of my brain won out. Mind you, it's not like I had to wake up super early to attend church. It was 7:15 when I got up! I really have no excuse for not going to Mass every day.

I'm sure glad I went. During the consecration I had a basic but powerful thought. It's not a profound or new concept, but it struck me nonetheless. When we receive Christ in the Eucharist, we become holy. We receive Jesus, who is holy, into our bodies physically, so we become holy. It was a great reminder for me. If I'm holy because Jesus is within me, I need to act accordingly. I should be appropriately reverent.

I remember a simple action that my late wife, Jean, would do after every Mass. As soon as she got home, Jean would drink a glass of water. She would not consume any food or drink until she drank that glass of water. She wanted to make sure that she didn't disrespect Jesus by consuming food immediately after receiving Him. It was a simple act of devotion, but one with profound meaning that I'm sure Jesus loved. As with many of Jean's practices, I'm now doing the same thing. Jean understood that when she received the body of Jesus in the Eucharist she became holy, and she acted accordingly.

It's the same with us. When we receive Jesus in the Eucharist, we become holy, at least for a time. The length of time that we remain holy is up to us. The Eucharist is not like other food we eat, where we digest it, consume the nutrients and it's gone a little while later. No. With the Eucharist, Jesus remains – for as long as we want Him to. He remains, and we remain holy until we forget that He dwells within us, and we commit a sin. In other words, we're holy until we decide we're not. If we remind ourselves to respond to Him with reverence, we will stand a greater chance of remaining holy for longer.

Furthermore, I think the more frequently we receive Communion, the more likely this holiness will take root and become lasting. Hopefully it becomes more of a reminder each time. Athletes use the term "muscle memory." The more you practice something – say, hitting a baseball – the more it becomes natural because the brain and the muscles remember it. It should be the same way with our longing for Christ and desire to be holy. The more often we receive His body and reflect on the fact that His presence in us makes us holy, the more likely it is that this condition will take root in our souls.

I once heard a priest say that when we receive holy Communion we experience the Divine and are with those in Heaven, even if just briefly. We are in the presence of the saints, all of them. We also are in the presence of our loved ones, including in my case, Jean. And they are rejoicing! They are rejoicing because they know firsthand the power of the Eucharist. Jesus' sacrifice on the Cross and their participation in that sacrifice every time they received Communion helped them get to Heaven. So yes, they truly are rejoicing – for themselves and for us, for they know that every time we receive the Eucharist, we get a little closer to our ultimate goal of being in Heaven and reunited with them.

September 27, 2022

FINDING THE MESSIAH

To be with Him we must be willing to put aside the concerns of our daily lives, our worries, our desires, our inward focus and give ourselves over to Jesus, even if it's just for a short period.

Today's Gospel describes the scene when John the Baptist and his disciples encounter Jesus. Upon seeing Jesus, John exclaims, "Behold, the lamb of God!" (John 1:36). Two of John's disciples then leave him to follow Jesus. One of them, Andrew, rushes home and tells his brother Simon (Peter), "We have found the Messiah." (John 1:41) How thrilling this must have been for Andrew! The Jewish people were very familiar with Scripture, so presumably Andrew knew about the prophecies concerning the Savior who was to come. Imagine his excitement upon realizing that everything he had heard about was being fulfilled in his midst. And, of course, we know that Andrew and Peter would go on to become Apostles of Jesus.

If we take a moment to put ourselves into this scene, it's not hard to feel Andrew's excitement – it must have been palpable. In our spiritual journey, we also are seeking the Messiah. From Scripture, we know that Jesus came and lived among us 2,000 years ago. We know He suffered, died on a cross and rose from the dead. We know He ascended into Heaven, and once He was there, God sent the Holy Spirit so Jesus could continue to dwell among us, even today. So why do I say we are still seeking the Messiah? At least in my case, my faith journey is very much an iterative process. On some days I feel like I'm on the right path, but on many others I struggle to find Him. He's always there, but there's too much "noise" in my life – in my mind – that often prevents me from finding Him.

At their first encounter Jesus says to Andrew and the others, "What are you looking for?" (John 1:38). The disciples give an interesting answer: "Rabbi, where do you stay?" (John 1:38). Their answer implies that they had immediately put their trust in Him and wanted to be with Him.

What are we looking for when we seek Jesus? How do we answer the question? Do we want to be with Him? I think we all would answer "Yes." However, deep down, is that really our answer? To be with Him we must be willing to put aside the concerns of our daily lives, our worries, our desires, our inward focus and give ourselves over to Jesus, even if it's just for a short period. For me that's much more difficult than it should be. I desire to get closer to God and to spend time with Him each day but I'm too easily distracted. How can I change that?

Intellectually, the answer is simple. When we're looking for something – when we really want something – that thing moves to the top of our mind. We focus on it over everything else. And when we achieve it, we're thrilled.

I think back to the year I was up for election to the partnership of my public accounting firm. I had spent my career with the firm up to that point and had worked extremely hard. Early in the year, I was told that I was "on the list" for the partnership. I was filled with both excitement and anxiety. This had been my goal for a long time and now it was within reach. I really wanted it and worked even harder during the year to make sure I was doing everything in my power to achieve my goal. It was at the top of my mind all year long. When I got the call informing me that I had made partner, I was ecstatic. I thanked God and called my family and friends to tell them the good news. I don't think my feet touched the ground for the rest of the day!

Andrew's reaction was probably similar, but in his case the prize was much, much greater. He had been taught about the Messiah since he was young, and he therefore was probably vigilant for signs of His coming. When he realized that he had found Him, he rejoiced and ran home to share the good news with his brother.

Andrew is a good example to follow in our faith journey. He had a normal job just like us, but he never lost sight of what he was seeking. Because of his focus, when he encountered Jesus, Andrew realized He was the Messiah. In response, he rejoiced and shared the good news with others. Let's emulate Andrew and we too will say, "We have found the Messiah."

January 4, 2023

JESUS' PEACE

Instead of spending our days worrying about things that, in the end, are not important, how much better would it be to spend that time treasuring this gift of peace?

Lately I've been feeling like a hamster running on a wheel who can't stop. Life has been particularly busy, and on top of that there have been some things that have been causing me stress. No matter how hard I try I can't seem to relax. Inevitably, at some point every day I yearn for a little peace and quiet.

Today I decided to try and do something about it. I stopped looking at my to-do list and took time for quiet reflection. I tried to calm my mind and become open to the presence of Christ. More often than not, when I attempt to do this, I'm not successful because I'm unable to truly open myself up to let Jesus in. As we know, Jesus is always near, but He won't force Himself in (sometimes I wish He would), but He will always respond if we let Him. Today was one of my better days. I was able to clear my mind of the daily clutter for just a few minutes and what a gift I received. While I sat in quiet solitude, a simple thought came into my mind. It was simple but profound, and just one word – peace. It changed my entire outlook.

As I listened, I heard Jesus tell me to reflect on His peace. When I did I became incredibly relaxed. I've been more tense than usual lately so this was exactly what I needed.

And that shouldn't be surprising – God <u>always</u> provides what we need. The message from Jesus was subtle and simple, which is why it's so important to stop the daily activity for just a few minutes and focus on Him. It's likely that Jesus had been trying to convey this message to me for several days but I wasn't listening because I was distracted by other things.

It's the ultimate irony, right? We're so anxious about what's going on in our lives that we can't find any time to be with Jesus. However, if we did take that time – and it only needs to be a few minutes each day — we would be less worried, and that would free our minds to face our daily challenges with greater focus. The peace of Christ is a profound gift – so profound that we as humans cannot comprehend it. We need God's help for that too. Thankfully, we have another even more important gift that's there for us whenever we need it. And it's really close to us. In fact, it's within us – Jesus, who dwells in our souls. All we have to do is open our minds and our hearts to Him.

One related thought. I spent my quiet time today sitting in front of the crucifix in my room. When I finished, I looked up at the crucifix and was struck by this fact: This peace that only Jesus can provide was purchased at a very high price – His life. Jesus gave His life so that we could live in the peace of knowing that we don't have to worry about ours. Because of His sacrifice, we are now heirs to God's kingdom. Thus, this gift of peace is very precious. Instead of spending our days worrying about things that, in the end, are not important, how much better would it be to spend that time treasuring this gift of peace? I think we all would trade anxiety and despair for peace and joy any day.

April 10, 2022

PAUL E. TUPPER

HE NEVER GIVES UP

*...no matter how many times we fall short,
Jesus will never give up on us. Ever.*

As children we implicitly trust our parents. Long before we understand why, we simply know they will always be there for us. As a kid I never worried about whether breakfast or dinner would be on the table; I just knew my mom would make something. I never thought about why we had a roof over our heads or a car to drive in; I just knew my dad would provide.

The same was true on the emotional side. I never even gave a moment's thought as to who I would turn to when I had a bad day; it always was mom (dad was usually at work). No matter what was going on I could go to her, and she knew exactly what to say. She always made me feel better. When I got cut from the sports team or did poorly on a test, she was always there to comfort me. More importantly, she never gave up on me. And as I got older, I realized this was the reason why I had always trusted her implicitly: She never gave up on me. I'm convinced that her faith in me – and later in my life, my wife's faith in me – shaped my inner core and helped to drive the success I was able to achieve.

We have a Savior who never gives up on us either. For years, God sent prophets to the Israelites to try to turn them from their sinful ways. It didn't work; they continued to turn away from God. But God never gave up. Eventually, God sent His only Son to live among them and provide firsthand teaching, pleading with the Jewish people to repent and follow His words. They didn't. Still, God never gave up.

Ultimately, God asked His Son to give His life so that all of us could be saved. Jesus said yes to His Father. An innocent man totally without sin, He subjected Himself to false accusations, torture and a horrific death so we could be saved. Jesus gave His very life for us. He didn't give up on us.

Jesus still doesn't give up on us. Even though we all turn away from Him at one time or another, He never turns away from us. He is always there. We can trust Him. He will never give up on us. He will never let go of us. We need to make sure that we don't let go of Him.

I have a tendency to repeat the same sins over and over again. Maybe we all do. I ask God for forgiveness and try to change my ways, but before long I've done it again. If I'm being honest, I probably know before I even ask for forgiveness that I'm going to fail again. That fact makes me wonder whether Jesus really will forgive me. I say to myself – Jesus made the ultimate sacrifice for me; He must be upset with me. I don't deserve to be forgiven.

The truth is I don't deserve to be forgiven. None of us do. And that's precisely the point. We don't deserve what Jesus did for us by dying on the Cross. Then why did He die for us? Because He didn't give up on us. And no matter how many times we fall short, Jesus will never give up on us. Ever. He will always welcome us back with open arms, just like the Father in the parable of the Prodigal Son. And if we believe in His mercy and His love, we will be successful in our life's journey back to God.

It's not up to Him. He already made His decision. It's up to us.

August 2, 2023

THANK GOD FOR MOMS

Jesus' Mother is also our Mother. Just as our moms watch out for us, just as they take care of us, just as they will do anything for us, it's the same with our Blessed Mother.

The minute my mom walked into the hospital room I knew I was going to be okay. It had started out as a typical day for an eight-year-old boy. I was playing outside with my best friend Duane. Just beyond our backyard there was a new house being built. We were playing cops and robbers, and I was the cop chasing Duane through the site. My foot got caught in a rut and I fell – hard. My arm hit a concrete block when I landed. I had never felt such pain in my life.

As fate would have it, both of my parents were out of town that day. Fortunately, Duane's mom was home and took me to the hospital. Thank God for moms. An x-ray determined that I had a spiral fracture of my arm, just above the elbow. For some crazy reason the doctor kept moving my arm around, which caused excruciating pain. Finally he left the room to look after another patient. I was trying my best to hold back the tears because even crying caused pain. I was miserable.

After what seemed like forever but really was only a few

minutes, my mom burst into the room and ran over to me. She hugged me tightly, carefully avoiding the injured arm. I hung on to her for dear life. There was no way I was letting go. Mom whispered that she loved me and that everything was going to be fine. I immediately relaxed – because she was there and would take care of me. Mom always made things better. Thank God for moms.

There were countless other times when my mom made everything okay. Similarly, I'm sure my son Paul can point to numerous times when his mom made everything okay for him. It's not an exaggeration to say that Jean made it a core mission of her life to make sure everything was good with Paul. Thank God for moms.

Today the Church celebrates the Feast of the Assumption so it's fitting to be reflecting upon mothers. All mothers want the best for their kids. All mothers absorb the sorrows and worries of their children.

It's the same with our Blessed Mother. She observed the miracles Jesus performed and watched as the crowds reacted in wonder. In fact, she compelled Jesus to perform His first miracle. She also witnessed the sorrows and worries of Jesus. She was there when the villagers brought Jesus to the precipice at the end of town, intending to throw Him off the cliff (Luke 4). She was at the foot of the Cross to witness Jesus' death. And she was also there a few days later to witness His Resurrection.

Jesus led a very busy life. He was always on the move, both to preach the Good News and to stay ahead of those who wanted to kill Him. I'm sure He turned to His Mother often for comfort, love and strength. Even though He was God, Jesus was human like us. He needed His mom, and She was there for Him. Thank God for moms.

Jesus' Mother is also our Mother. Just as our moms watch out for us, just as they take care of us, just as they will do anything for us, it's the same with our Blessed Mother. She knows how precious we are in the eyes of Her Son, and so we're precious in her eyes as well. She shares our joys and she feels our sorrows. She worries about us. She wants us to be good Christians and to get to Heaven, and She will intercede unceasingly on our behalf to help us get there.

I'm sure we all can remember how fiercely our mothers protected us when we were young. Mary does the same thing for us throughout our lives. She fiercely protects us from the evil one. And she is our strongest intercessor with Her Son. We should pray to Her and be sure to thank Her every day. We cannot fathom the depth of the love that Jesus and our Blessed Mother have for each of us. Thank God for moms.

August 15, 2024

THEY DOUBTED

So is all hope lost for us when we doubt Jesus? The short answer is no. Like the Apostles, we're not perfect, but Jesus will never give up on us just like He never gave up on the Apostles.

"The eleven disciples went to Galilee, to the mountain which Jesus had ordered them. When they all saw him, they worshiped, but they doubted." (Matthew 28:16-17).

They doubted. The Apostle doubted. It doesn't make any sense. After everything they had witnessed how could they still doubt that Jesus was God? This is the last scene in Gospel of Matthew. By this time the Apostles had spent three years with Jesus. They had observed His miracles; they had heard His teachings.

They saw Him get arrested. When He was led away, they abandoned Him. Yes, they doubted then – every one of them, despite all that they had witnessed for three years.

Then, three days later, Jesus rose from the dead. The Apostles witnessed that too. Jesus appeared to them on multiple occasions after the Resurrection. Even Thomas, who had missed one of those occasions, and as a result, needed assurance, proclaimed Jesus as Lord upon seeing Him a week later. Surely, they couldn't possibly doubt any more. But they did. Even Thomas.

Why? The answer is simple. The Apostles, like us, were human. Yes, they were handpicked by Jesus. They were witnesses to His life. They saw His power and even manifested some of it themselves. They had every advantage, but still they were human, and that means they couldn't do it on their own. Even though Jesus called them and personally prepared them for their mission, the task was beyond their capacity to fulfill on their own.

If the Apostles, who had lived with Jesus and witnessed His resurrection, still had doubts, what hope is there for us? If these men who were personally chosen by Jesus struggled with their faith, what is the way forward for us?

Jesus was fully aware of the Apostles' doubt. He could have been angry or at least disappointed in them after all the time they had spent together. No one would have blamed Him for such a reaction. Jesus' response, however, was not anger but encouragement and hope – the ultimate expression of hope for them and for us. He commissioned them to spread the Gospel and left them with these parting words: "Behold, I am with you always, until the end of the age." (Matthew 28:20).

Jesus promised the doubters to be with them always. But Jesus went further. Although the Apostles didn't realize it at the time, His promise wasn't just to be with them – He would dwell within them. Jesus fulfilled this promise on Pentecost Sunday when He came down upon them through the Holy Spirit.

That's when everything truly changed for the Apostles. Their doubt went away, and their fears were erased. They began to speak out boldly in the name of Jesus. With the guidance and strength from the Holy Spirit, they fulfilled the mission Jesus had commissioned them for.

Jesus provides the same hope for us. He dwells within each of us through the Holy Spirit. His Spirit gives us the strength we need to accomplish what we otherwise could not do on own – to live Christian lives, to follow His teachings, to fulfill His mission.

So is all hope lost for us when we doubt Jesus? The short answer is no. Like the Apostles, we're not perfect, but Jesus will never give up on us just like He never gave up on the Apostles. If the Apostles doubted and Jesus still made them leaders of the early church, there is hope for us. If we believe that Jesus dwells within us and we trust the Holy Spirit for guidance, we should have nothing but hope. Jesus will never leave us. He promised. And Jesus always keeps His promises.

"Behold, I am with you always, until the end of the age."

May 28, 2024

JESUS' ANGER

Jesus is upset with us because He loves us so much and has shown us how to ensure that we'll be with Him always, and too often we don't respond ⁻ at least I don't.

Have you ever been in a situation where someone was angry with you because you didn't understand what he or she was asking you to do? I certainly have. It seemed so clear to the other person, but it just didn't click for me.

There was an instance early in my career where the partner asked me to write a memo summarizing the results of our team's work in a certain area. He gave me some general guidance and sent me on my way. It was near the end of the audit, so time was of the essence. I was both nervous and excited. The partner had come straight to me with his request. He didn't ask the manager to write the memo; he asked me, a younger staff member! I wanted to do a really good job to affirm his confidence in me. I labored on the memo into the wee hours of the morning and put it in on his desk for his review as I left to grab a few hours of sleep.

The next day I overheard the partner saying to the manager, "What is this? I gave Paul a simple assignment, and he didn't produce what I asked for. I don't think he gets it!" I was crestfallen. I thought I had understood what the partner wanted and had worked hard on the memo. However, I clearly didn't comprehend his guidance and had missed the mark. The partner was upset with me. I thought for sure my career was over.

Today's Gospel reading from Matthew depicts Jesus as angry (Matthew, Chapter 11). He reproaches the towns like Capernaum where He had worked miracles because His works had not swayed the people to repent. We don't see Jesus upset too often in the Gospels, so when we do it makes sense to pay attention. When I heard this passage in the past I hadn't grasped the full sense of His frustration. I always had thought of it as a sobering passage, but I didn't think much beyond that.

Today it hit me immediately. Jesus is really upset here. And it makes sense. His purpose for coming into the world was to convince people to repent, believe in Him and be saved. He worked numerous miracles. The people reacted with wonder, but the majority did not change their lives. These people had witnessed God in the flesh – they saw Him and the works He did. However, they did not have a change of heart. Jesus wanted them to repent, so He understandably was upset at their unwillingness to change.

Is it the same for us? As I reflected on this passage, I thought that I'm like them much of the time, unfortunately. Granted, Jesus hasn't performed any miracles that I've personally witnessed, and that's probably the case for most of us. We haven't met Him in human form like the folks in Capernaum did. But unlike them, we have the Gospels that capture Jesus' words and message to all of us. We also have the examples of "saints" we each have known who demonstrated what it's like to repent and truly know

Christ. And we have the Risen Jesus who dwells within us, who is constantly there to provide guidance as to how we can and should live our lives.

In sum, the truth is we may not be much different from the people of Capernaum. We hear the word of God, but most of the time we go about living our lives as we always have. Jesus' words are addressed to us as well as the folks in those towns 2,000 years ago. Jesus is upset with us because He loves us so much and has shown us how to ensure that we'll be with Him always, and too often we don't respond – at least I don't. It bears repeating: He is upset with us because He loves us so much.

As Jeff Smith wrote in his reflection today in *The Word Among Us*: "God loves you and will do anything to get your attention when you stray, even if it means a harsh rebuke." (*The Word Among Us*, July 2022: p. 33).

The partner certainly got my attention with his words to the manager on that day many years ago. My response was to start over and try to do it correctly the next time, which fortunately I did. Jesus gives us a second chance too. Let's react to the anger he expresses in today's Gospel – anger that is as much directed to us today as it was to the people of Capernaum – by really listening to His words to us and repenting and following Him.

July 12, 2022

DON'T BLUR THE LINES

Jesus told us that the gate to Heaven is narrow. It seems to me that when we think it's ok to just do the minimum, that gate becomes even narrower.

During my career I occasionally worked with colleagues who did the bare minimum day after day. They never went the extra mile to ease the burden on a stressed colleague. They never pitched in to help the team get a project completed sooner. These people came in at nine and left at five – every day. It was tempting to be envious of them because they no doubt had a better lifestyle than those of us who stayed late. They seemed to have it all. And maybe in the short term, they did.

Reflecting on it now, these colleagues did not have long careers with our firm. They presumably came to realize that they were not going to progress up the promotion track if they weren't willing to put in the extra work. So they left to do something else.

Recently at Mass, the priest commented that too often we as Christians think that doing the minimum is enough. That got me thinking. How many of us in our spiritual lives are like those colleagues at work? It's tempting to say that going to Mass on Sunday is enough to fulfill our obligations as followers of Christ. We all lead busy lives, and those busy lives have expanded into our weekends. For example, for those with children, there are often athletic or other weekend events so that sometimes it's hard to even make it to church, much less take time to volunteer, read Scripture, say the Rosary, or do anything else in service to God.

The problem is that if we adopt this attitude, we risk the same fate as those work colleagues. We will not advance in our spiritual journey. Only in this case, the stakes are a lot higher. Those work colleagues were able to get other jobs to support themselves and their families. With God, there is no alternative. We're either advancing toward Heaven or we're not. Fortunately we have a merciful God who will welcome us back every time we drift in our faith and ask for His forgiveness. But we need to be careful. Jesus told us that the gate to Heaven is narrow. It seems to me that when we think it's ok to just do the minimum, that gate becomes even narrower.

I do have to say that sometimes it can be confusing for me. We hear quite often that doing little things for God and others can matter. Saint Therese of Lisieux (the Little Flower) said that little things can produce big results when we do them for God. This is where we must be careful not to blur the lines. God rejoices at every little act we do for Him. However, there's a big difference between doing something small versus doing the bare minimum for Him.

The fundamental difference is in our attitude. We should be thankful to God for all that He has given us, most especially the gift of eternal life attained by the sacrifice of His Son. That should make us want to spend time with Him and to approach our lives with an attitude of charity. When we have this mindset, we show our love for God. We're doing the things we do because we want to, not because we think we have to. Invariably there will be days when we can't do much, and God understands that. On those days, the little things mean even more to God because we took time we really didn't have to respond to Him.

Let's pray that the Holy Spirit helps us to discern the difference between doing the minimum and doing the little things. Our salvation depends on it.

July 25, 2023

IT'S NOT ABOUT ME

God's calling is not about me. It's about Him and doing His will.

For someone who strives to be modest in life, I have a tendency to make it all about me. When Jean and I were having an argument about something (thankfully, this was a rare occurrence), she would say "You're making it about you again. This is not about you." Man, that used to get under my skin! But with the benefit of hindsight – and perhaps some guidance from the Holy Spirit – I realized that Jean was right.

Too often, my immediate reaction to a situation is to make it about me and my needs. That might be true for many of us. Recently I've realized that God is trying to help me recognize this flaw and to remedy it.

Here are a few simple examples of how, even with little things, we can inadvertently make it about ourselves. A few weeks ago, I was coming out of the grocery store near my apartment in New York City. There was a homeless man sitting on the corner with a jar for donations. He's there frequently so I was ready with my money. As I was about to put it in his jar, I noticed that he was looking down at the ground and didn't see me. I hesitated because, subconsciously, I think I wanted him to notice me putting cash in his jar. Then I realized what I was doing. By wanting him to see me, I was making it about me.

Later that week I returned to my apartment after a walk. I got to the elevator and pushed the button. While I was waiting another resident came into the lobby. The person had a mask on so I figured she was concerned about Covid. I offered to let her take the first elevator, and I would wait for the next one. She got on the elevator and went up. What she didn't do was thank me for letting her go first. Instead of shrugging it off, knowing that I had done a very small but good deed, I got annoyed that she didn't thank me. I had let it become about me.

A daily Gospel passage recently was about Jesus commissioning the twelve Apostles. While reflecting on the passage, I thought about what God is calling me to do for Him. Through the Holy Spirit's inspiration, God is calling me to become a better student of Scripture by reading and studying it more intently. Furthermore, I believe He is calling me to minister to others through my writing.

It's a great feeling to think that, with my writing, I'm doing God's will. However, occasionally, I'll start to think that it's important that my writing be accepted by others. With those thoughts, I make it about me. Even with the ministry that God is calling me to do, I can manage to make it about me.

This realization put my feet back on the ground. God's calling is not about me. It's about Him and doing His will. At the end of the day it doesn't matter whether others approve of my writing. I'm writing for God, and He has a plan for me. He will determine how my writing will be used to accomplish His plans. I need to remember that it's about God, not me.

An excerpt from a book I'm reading captures well what I've been experiencing. In his *In the School of the Holy Spirit*, Jacques Philippe writes, "When we are moved by the Holy Spirit, there may well be (because we are human) some little thought of vainglory that starts to grow in us like a parasite (and that we should fight against), but deep down we see very clearly that we are not only weak, that all good we can do comes from God, and that we have precisely nothing to boast about." (p. 55).

In my case, God is the author, not me. All credit goes to Him through the Holy Spirit. It's the same for all of us. It's not about us. It's about God.

August 29, 2021

RETURNING TO WORK, SCHOOL...AND GOD

> *...when we receive Holy Communion we are returning to Jesus. To be specific, every time we go to Mass and receive the Eucharist, we have made a decision (even if subconsciously) to return to Jesus.*

It's the end of August, and people are returning to their normal routines. At Mass this morning I noticed a large group of people filing in just before the start of the ceremony. The priest welcomed them and explained that the St. Mary School teachers were back for the start of the school year. Today, Jessica returned to work, having finished her vacation. Today, my nephew started his first day of college – at Yale! It seemed there were fewer people in the grocery store, presumably because vacations were over. Summer is coming to an end, and people are returning to work and school.

As I observed this today, I thought: Our faith journey isn't much different. While our goal is to be on the path to God at all times, the reality for many of us—certainly me—is that we occasionally take a break, so to speak. We stray from the path. In my case, it can happen several times each day. I know that God doesn't expect us to be focused on Him all the time (thankfully). He understands our limitations. But I certainly should be able to remain focused during the times I've set aside to be with Him. Daily Mass takes less than 30 minutes, but too often I'm thinking about something else that I need to do. The Rosary takes about 15 minutes to pray, but I frequently find my thoughts wandering. I can't even focus for a few minutes, which then makes me frustrated.

Fortunately, we have a God who is patient and infinitely merciful. He's always happy when we turn, or return, to Him. Jesus is the shepherd who will leave the 99 sheep in the flock to find the one who strayed, and then rejoices when that one returns. Every time we stray or become distracted He will always welcome us back.

During the Mass, I realized that when we receive Holy Communion we are returning to Jesus. When we've strayed, going to Communion is going to Jesus – literally. That's why I've formed a habit of saying the Act of Contrition before I receive the Host. It helps me to refocus on Him and prepares my soul to receive Him.

Not only does Jesus welcome us back, He rejoices when we come back to Him. But there's still more. Despite us turning away from Him, not only does He forgive us, Jesus actually gives us a gift – Himself, in Holy Communion. We turned away from the One who gave His life for us; when we return, He gives Himself to us again. The depth of God's mercy simply doesn't make sense in the self-righteous world we live in. Fortunately, we don't have to understand it. We just need to believe and accept this wonderful gift.

At this time of year when we're returning to our routines, let's return to God as well. Better yet, let's look to bring God more fully into our daily routines, so His love can radiate from us to those we interact with.

August 23, 2022

PAUL E. TUPPER

MENTORS AND ADVOCATES

> *...each of us has a plethora of mentors we can look to for our spiritual development. But who is our advocate? The answer is clear: Jesus, through His Holy Spirit, is our Advocate.*

I spent my entire career working for a public accounting firm – thirty-four years with the same company. When I mention that, most people look at me as if I were a dinosaur. And that's probably how they think of me – no one works for the same firm for that long these days. I <u>was</u> a dinosaur! When I reflect on my career, though, I'm both humbled and proud of what I accomplished.

Recently, someone asked me to name the key success factors to my career. I think the person expected me to say hard work, a bit of luck or the like. While those were contributors, my answer was different. By far, the factor that had the greatest impact on my success was mentoring. At every step of my career – right up to the end – I had terrific mentors and advocates.

A mentor was someone always available to give counsel – immediate advice about a pressing client issue, near-term advice about which client I should take on next, or long-term advice about how best to advance my career prospects.

As I mentioned, I had a mentor during every stage of my career. I could always turn to him/her, and that person would make time for me. They were invested in me. As I progressed in my own career, I did my best to mentor others. I drew on the examples of my mentors to try and help me to be a better mentor in turn.

An advocate's role is different. An advocate is someone who, to use a sports analogy, will "go to bat" for you. My advocate tried to make sure I was viewed well by the firm's leadership and worked actively to advance my career. As opposed to a mentor who helped me help myself in my career, my advocate acted directly on my behalf. While my mentor guided me in thinking through which clients would be best from a developmental perspective, my advocate helped to get me on those clients. He was able to influence the decisions because he was in a leadership position.

So what does any of this have to do with our spirituality? Hopefully we have mentors in our spiritual lives. There are certainly plenty to choose from. The Apostles can function as mentors for every one of us. They were like us in more ways than we may think. Yes, they were able to experience Jesus in human form, which none of us can do. However, like us, their faith wavered, and they doubted, even though Jesus was present physically with them. Ultimately, they overcame their shortfalls, and formed the church. In the end, it was their faith and their perseverance that led to their success. We can pray to them for guidance and look to their lives for inspiration.

The Apostles were helped in a major way by their advocate. Their advocate was the Advocate – The Holy Spirit. Nothing they accomplished would have been possible without the Holy Spirit guiding and helping them. He was pulling for them to succeed.

In addition to the Apostles, we can turn to multiple sources for guidance – clergy, teachers, co-workers, spouses, to name a few. For me, I rely on multiple mentors for my spiritual development. I look to the Apostles and saints for the examples they set. I turn to the priest and deacon in my parish. I was heavily influenced by my mom and still am – I owe her a debt of gratitude as she was instrumental in the development of my faith. As is clearly evident from numerous examples in my writings, I look to my late wife, Jean. The way she lived her life is my roadmap toward being a good Christian. Finally, I draw inspiration from Jessica. Her quiet but steadfast faith and constant motivation have played a major role in the development of my faith over the past couple of years.

In sum, each of us has a plethora of mentors we can look to for our spiritual development. But who is our advocate? The answer is clear: Jesus, through His Holy Spirit, is our Advocate. He's constantly pulling for us. He will influence how we live our lives if we let Him. And have no doubt, if we believe in Him and try to live our lives according to His will, He will go to bat for us with His Father.

May 8, 2023

MY NEW BOSS

I have the best boss I could ever hope for. In fact, I have the perfect boss. We all do.

I've been retired for a little over two years. I'm still adjusting to my new life after a thirty-four-year career in public accounting. I like to tell myself that I'm working for God now. In that case, Jesus is my boss. Every morning when I wake up, I ask God to help me perform at a high level for Him during the day. I said the same words every day before I started work. However, my performance has not been very consistent in my new "job."

In my career as an accountant, I generally received good performance reviews. I worked hard and I stayed focused. In fact, I think my ability to focus was a core competency. That skill was particularly important later in my career because I would encounter multiple challenges and issues on a daily basis.

In retirement, I often have difficulty focusing, especially during my time with God, whether while writing, in prayer, at Mass or just in quiet reflection. I'm quite certain that, if an objective person were to give me a performance review on my work for God thus far, it would not be a positive one. I can visualize the comments now: "Paul has trouble focusing." "He's not being efficient." "He easily falls behind on his work product."

Admittedly, when I was working, there were deadlines, and they certainly helped to keep me on track. But that's not the only factor here. The main issue is that I'm not properly prioritizing. I have various activities that I do in a given day. Among them is my work for God, and I'm simply not carving out enough time for these activities.

In my career, my job almost always took priority over all other activities – sometimes to a fault. I need to adopt that same attitude in my spiritual work. Admittedly, the work for God can't become a burden, because if my heart's not in it the result won't be good. However, I'm confident that working for God will not become burdensome. I like what God is calling me to do. And I love my new boss!

The solution actually is quite simple and is familiar to me – after all, it was one of my core competencies for thirty-four years. If I prioritize my new career, it will become the focus of my day. Since I really like what I'm doing, it should not be difficult. In fact, I got some very good advice from my significant other. Jessica suggested that I do my work for God earlier in the day before disruptions occur and everyday life happens. So now, I start the day off by attending Mass, and then I focus on my writing as soon as I get home.

There's another element that should facilitate success in my new career – my boss. The importance of having a good supervisor can't be overstated. I was fortunate to have great managers/mentors when I was coming up the ranks in my accounting firm, and they had a more profound impact on my success by far than any other factor. Well, now I have the best boss I could ever hope for. In fact, I have the perfect boss. We all do.

For starters, He puts up with all our shortcomings. Not

only does He put up with them, He hired us knowing in advance all of our performance issues. If, in my previous career, my performance was as inconsistent, any objective performance manager would have probably fired me. Fortunately for me – and for all of us – God is not an objective performance manager. He's biased. He's biased toward us because He loves us so much. He's compassionate, and He will constantly provide guidance through His Holy Spirit to help us improve. All we have to do is ask Him for help and be attentive to His response.

Jesus, help me to work at a high level today for You.

January 26, 2023

PAUL E. TUPPER

MULTI-TASKING WITH GOD

We should strive to keep Jesus on in our minds and periodically remind ourselves of His presence throughout the day. In fact, we can think of Jesus as our virtual screen saver - or, more accurately, our life saver.

People talk about multi-tasking quite often these days. Everyone is super-busy with so many responsibilities, and we refer to multi-tasking as if it's the solution to the problem of not having enough time. I certainly know that I've said it numerous times – "I have a conference call this afternoon, but I also have a document to review, so I'll multi-task during the call." Frequently we say it as a badge of honor – as if we're somehow better than our colleagues because we're able to do several things at once.

I recently read that, in fact, true multi-tasking is impossible – that the brain can only focus on one task at a time. Further, if one is thinking about something else while performing a certain task, that person is not actually focused on the task at hand. I don't know if this is true, but it makes sense to me. I certainly can say that I've never been very efficient when I have attempted to multi-task.

However, there is one area where I do believe we can

multi-task, and that's our relationship with God. In *Jesus Always*, Sarah Young writes (in the person of Jesus), "My presence can bless you always – even when it's only in the background of your mind. You can learn to stay conscious of me while you are engaged in other matters." (*Jesus Always*, p. 200). What an amazing concept! While we're going about the craziness of our daily lives, we keep Jesus on in the background. And I'm sure He's content to be in the background of our minds most of the time.

Of course, there will need to be times when our focus must be fully on Him – when we're at Mass, praying or reading Scripture, to name a few. But if we can strive to always have Jesus on in the background, we can more readily turn to Him during the day: for a quick petition, to share our thoughts, to say thank you. Furthermore, if Jesus is already in the background, we can quickly bring Him to the forefront of our minds when we need His presence in our lives.

How is it possible to multi-task with God when we can't do it with any other subject? There is a simple answer – when we multi-task with God, the Holy Spirit is present, even if it's just in the background. So, in fact, we can't do it on our own. We need God's help.

Jesus is always close by – He dwells within us. We would do well to have a reminder of that as we go through each day, and multi-tasking with Him in the background is a good way to facilitate it. Another analogy might be the screen savers on our computers. They may be in the background, but they are always there as a reminder. Our screen saver could be a picture of our favorite vacation spot that brings back a good memory. It may be a message about cyber security to remind us to be cautious. Either way, our screen savers serve a dual purpose: They keep our computers on and display an image of something we want to or should keep in mind.

Continuing with the screen saver analogy, we should strive to keep Jesus on in our minds and periodically remind ourselves of His presence throughout the day. In fact, we can think of Jesus as our virtual screen saver – or, more accurately, our life saver – and make sure He's always in our thoughts.

August 5, 2022

RECHARGE TIME

...Jesus continually longs for us to have quiet time with Him. He wants us to take time to recharge our spiritual lives as well as our everyday lives.

Our jobs today are increasingly demanding. Companies want to do more with less, and thus expect us to be more productive. That, in turn, can wear us down. Occasionally, after a particularly tough stretch at work, I would say to my wife that I needed some recharge time. There were a number of ways to recharge: going away for a long weekend, going to the gym for a workout, or simply spending a quiet weekend at home to relax and catch up on sleep. In short, I needed something to build back my strength so I would be ready to go back at it, reenergized.

Let's face it – our lives are busy, and that's not going to change. I don't think I could count the number of times I've uttered the words, "My schedule is packed" or "I've got so much to do." And this is coming from someone who is retired! There is no doubt that we all need time to recharge. God thinks so too. In fact, Jesus continually longs for us to have quiet time with Him. He wants us to take time to recharge our spiritual lives as well as our everyday lives.

God provides numerous ways to recharge. We can read Scripture, pray the Rosary, attend Mass or simply spend quiet time in His presence. Any, or all, of these activities will help us to recharge our spiritual lives. They are meant to help us relax and renew our relationship with Jesus.

To help me work through the "busyness" of my daily life, I create to-do lists. These lists include activities to enhance my spiritual life, a combination of the items listed above. I recently realized, however, that these daily religious activities, because they're on my list, have contributed to this mindset that there are so many things I have to do. A few days ago I actually caught myself thinking, "Wow, I still have to work out, pay the bills and say the Rosary before I can get to my downtime for the day." That thought stopped me cold. Can you imagine – to think that praying is a chore? I realized that I'd had this mindset for a while. The part of my day that was meant to be my recharge/quiet time had become part of my "chores" for the day. Only I could manage to pull this one off!

God certainly doesn't want our time with Him to feel like an obligation. He desires us to spend as much time as we can with Him, but He, I'm sure, prefers it to happen because we want to be with Him, not because we think we have to. This realization flipped the script for me. It got me re-grounded to look forward to my daily time with Jesus as true recharge time – as relaxation time, not chore time. But there's more. By taking this time every day to be with Jesus and hopefully by taking some time to listen to Him, we strengthen our faith. We stand ready to receive any messages Jesus may be trying to send us. Most importantly, we deepen our relationship with Him. When you stop to think, that's quite an effective recharge – and it's free.

June 14, 2022

BEING ALIGNED

It all was in alignment, and I experienced a feeling of peace, not only peace, but happiness - even joy. It was truly remarkable, and it was a gift from God.

Today was one of those days (unfortunately, it doesn't happen often) where I seemed to be connected with Jesus. My faith, my relationship with Him and the events of my daily life all seemed to be in alignment. It's a phenomenal feeling. I first realized it on my walk to Mass. I was in New York and decided to take the scenic route along the Hudson River. Although it made the trip twice as long, it was a beautiful day and I wanted to enjoy it. As I started my walk, I was thinking about my values and wondering whether what I do on a given day lines up with those values. Then I thought about my decision to take the long way and realized that the answer might actually be "Yes."

The things that I do on a given day – exercise, attend Mass, spend time with my better half, pray, talk to family members, and write – all, in fact, do line up with my values. And the walk did too. I was spending quiet time where I could think, and I was doing it while getting fresh air and exercise.

During the walk, I felt the presence of God around me. It wasn't overt – it rarely is. However, today I was more aware of it. I could feel it in the gentle breeze coming off the water. I could see it with the beautiful views along the Hudson River – the Statue of Liberty off in the distance, the boats going by, the cities on the other side of the river. I could smell it in the gentle aroma of the salt air. I could hear it in the joyful screams of the children during their school recess. And I could feel it in the smiles of those walking by me along the promenade who were also enjoying this early spring day.

The acute awareness of God's presence in the world and in my life made me more thankful for all the blessings He has given me. It was no surprise, then, that during the walk, I found myself saying, "Thank you, Jesus" frequently. Attending Mass further sharpened my sense of closeness to Jesus. As such, I remained in a similar state of mind on my walk home. I felt like I was closer to Him than I had been in a while.

Finally, my experience came to a culmination about two hours later – in the most unexpected place. I had just boarded a train in Grand Central Terminal to head to Connecticut. As I took my seat, an amazing feeling literally permeated through me – both mind and body. I had this incredible sense that everything was in perfect alignment – my relationship with Jesus, my relationship with Mary (I typically say the Rosary on my train rides, which is what I was doing at the time), what God is calling me to do, my relationship with Jessica, my relationship with my son – everything. It all was in alignment, and I experienced a feeling of peace, not only peace, but happiness – even joy. It was truly remarkable, and it was a gift from God.

This feeling, particularly the physical part, faded with time. But the experience stuck with me and I think about it frequently. I realize that I'm human – I have many flaws –

so I can't expect to always be in this state of profound alignment. However, the elements that produced it today – ensuring that my daily activities line up with my values, taking quiet time to be with God, striving to be aware of His presence and being thankful (probably the most important) – are things I certainly can try to focus on every day.

These are things we all can focus on. The elements are not difficult and they're not time consuming. We can even do them in the midst of our daily activities. For instance, it only takes a few seconds to say "Thank you" to God. As I can attest from personal experience, the effort is well worth it. And if we're successful in this regard, being aligned might just happen more frequently for each of us.

March 5, 2022

KEEP IT SIMPLE

...the simple act of turning to Jesus gives us grace. And that grace, combined with Christ's peace, are the only tools we need to help us avoid sin.

I was in New York City yesterday and decided to go to confession and Mass. As I was preparing for my confession, I thought about how close I had felt to Jesus during my previous time in the City. I rent a small apartment in lower Manhattan. It is a quiet place for me, and there's a Dominican church nearby where I often attend Mass. These two factors help me to better connect with God, and I had really felt a closeness to Him on the previous trip.

The intervening days were a blur of travel – three places in five days, with a family wedding and other events taking up much of my time. Because of this, I didn't find the time to achieve same closeness to Jesus. I also let myself get anxious; traveling often brings on some stress for me. I was disappointed in myself and confessed these sins to the priest.

I was surprised by his response: "You're trying too hard." He then said if we're looking to find God, it's not going to happen. God seeks us out. We merely need to be ready and accept Him when He does.

Think about that. God seeks us out. We don't have to work hard to find Him. As a child, we were taught that God is everywhere, so it follows that it isn't difficult to find Him. However, it's even simpler than that. He's not just everywhere. He seeks us. He calls us to Him. We just need to listen and respond.

Once again, God intervened here. I was prompted by the Holy Spirit to go to Confession before Mass. I asked the Holy Spirit to help me examine my conscience in preparation. The Holy Spirit answered my prayer and guided me to acknowledge my sins. Through the Sacrament of Reconciliation, I received forgiveness of those sins. But I also received advice to help me be a better Christian going forward.

I tend to over-think things and unnecessarily complicate many situations. People might even describe me as an egghead. Clearly, I had been doing this in my relationship with God, as the priest pointed out. Sometime, not too long ago, I was gently reminded by Jesus to "keep it simple." I often think that I'm not doing enough: I'm not praying intently; I don't have enough reverence for the holy Eucharist; I don't adequately prepare for Confession; I don't concentrate sufficiently when I'm praying or reading the Bible; I don't do enough for others. The list goes on. And every one of these statements is true.

On my own, I'm not good enough. None of us are. However, as the priest reminded me, God doesn't focus on our shortcomings. We're all sinners. God certainly knows that. It's why He sent Jesus to save us and to dwell within us today. The point is that we should stop focusing on where we fall short and instead focus on the fact that Jesus is with us – dwelling within us.

When I do this – when I simply acknowledge Him – a sense of peace follows that puts me in a good place: a happy place. I think that's probably the case for all of us. Furthermore, the simple act of turning to Jesus gives us grace. And that grace, combined with Christ's peace, are the only tools we need to help us avoid sin.

We simply need to continually remind ourselves: "Don't try too hard. Keep it simple. Let God do the hard work." And He will. He wants to. As Jesus stated in Matthew's Gospel, "My yoke is easy, and my burden light." (Matthew 11:30).

August 22, 2021

ANXIETY

...we are reminded to constantly recognize that Jesus is right here with us to help us face any challenge, so we never need to be worried.

A recent Wall Street Journal (May 7, 2022) article caught my eye: "Can Anxiety Be Good for You?" I experience anxiety quite often – for the most part about trivial matters, if I'm being honest – so I was immediately intrigued. Wow. If anxiety can actually be good for you, I'd be a lucky man!

The gist of the article was that some level of anxiety can help in challenging situations. For example, if you're a bit worried about an upcoming job interview, you're likely to spend more time in preparation and, thus, may perform better. Certainly, during my working days, I felt anxiety before important client meetings – especially board meetings – and that caused me to spend hours in preparation. Undoubtedly, the extent of this preparation was much to the chagrin of my team members, as I repeatedly asked them to assemble various supporting materials to aid in responding to potential questions. As a result of the preparation, however, the meetings generally went well, perhaps supporting the article's hypothesis.

The article also made the point that we should pursue

excellence, not perfection. Once again, some level of anxiety probably will help us to work harder and be more focused, and that can help us to achieve excellence in what we're doing. On the other hand, no level of anxiety is going to help us achieve perfection. In fact, the pursuit of perfection will more likely lead to more anxiety.

While contemplating the conclusions from the article, I decided to watch a homily by Father Edward Meeks. The one I chose was entitled, "No Anxiety." (homily on YouTube, December 12, 2021). In his talk, Father Meeks provides a different take on anxiety. His talk refers us to St. Paul's letter to the Philippians (Philippians 4:4-6) where we are told to rejoice always in God and to dismiss all anxiety from our minds because Jesus is here, present with us.

If we really stopped to reflect on the fact that Jesus is right here with us, right now – that He actually dwells within us – why would we ever worry about anything? St. Paul sums it up in an amazing way. If we turn our fears over to God – if we dismiss them -- then "God's own peace, which is beyond all understanding, will stand guard over our hearts and minds, in Christ Jesus." (Philippians 4:7). These passages, by the way, are among my favorites in all the Bible.

I like this view of anxiety much more than the one in the newspaper article. I don't want to embrace anxiety! It was not a coincidence that I decided to listen to one of Father Meeks' homilies on the same day as the "anxiety" article in the newspaper.

In the end, we can learn something from both sources. From the Wall Street Journal article, we are encouraged to strive for excellence, not perfection. From Father Meeks' homily, we are reminded to constantly recognize that Jesus is right here with us to help us face any challenge, so we never need to be worried.

Any time we feel apprehensive, we can turn to Scripture. There will be a particular passage that can speak to us. For me, it's the above passage from Philippians. It always helps to get me to a better place. We can also go to the words of Jesus Himself. In addressing the Apostles for the last time before His suffering and death, He said to them, "Do not let your hearts be troubled. Have faith in God and faith in me." (John 14:1). Jesus is there for us and with us every time we feel anxious. It's up to us to put our faith in Him and give our anxieties over to Him, and then let His peace stand guard over our hearts and minds.

May 9, 2022

PAUL E. TUPPER

THE IMPORTANCE OF PRAYER

Jesus was in communion with God. That tells us that Jesus' prayer with God was not a one-way prayer. It was a dialogue between Him and His Father.

Prayer is a fundamental part of our spiritual lives. Most of us learn them when we are kids. As a family, we said the same "grace" each night before dinner. My mom taught me certain prayers to say at bedtime. Of course, as children many of us learned to recite the Lord's Prayer. To this day I continue to say many of the same prayers I learned long ago.

When we're facing a crisis, our prayers tend to become much more intense. We pour everything we have into our pleadings before Jesus. Several years ago, my father was in the hospital due to a stomach ulcer. We received a call just before midnight that there had been a rupture, and the doctors were immediately taking him into surgery to try and stop the bleeding. My mom and I rushed to the hospital. When we arrived, the staff informed us that the surgery was in progress and that there was a real possibility that my dad might not survive the procedure.

The surgery lasted almost four hours – some of the longest hours of my life. I can't even imagine what it must have been like for my mom. Fortunately, she had the foresight to bring a prayer book with her to the hospital. We spent much of those four hours in prayer – reading prayers from her book, reciting the Rosary and simply talking to Jesus, practically begging Him to help my dad through the surgery and to heal him. Our prayers were focused and intense.

After what seemed to be an eternity, the doctor came into the waiting room and gave us the news. Dad had come through the surgery and was expected to make a full recovery. My mom and I both breathed a huge sigh of relief. We were elated but also exhausted. It had been a long night, but Jesus had listened to and answered our prayers.

During the months of my late wife's illness, I similarly prayed with an intensity I normally don't have. I prayed frequently and fervently. I never gave up. I felt connected to God during those periods of prayer. I know God heard every one of my prayers. And He answered them, just not the way I had hoped He would. With the benefit of hindsight, however, God's answer was better for Jean. I think God wanted Jean with Him. He mercifully ended Jean's suffering and brought her to Heaven. How could I ever ask for more than that?

The concept of praying when we're encountering a crisis or before we face a major event is not new. In fact, we have guidance in the Gospels that encourages us to do just that. Jesus prayed constantly, but the Gospels tell us that He prayed with a more intense focus on certain occasions.

On Holy Thursday, Jesus faced a crisis. He knew what He was about to endure, and it was going to be awful. In response, He prayed – intently. In the Garden of Olives,

Luke writes "In his anguish he prayed with all the greater intensity, and his sweat became like drops of blood falling to the ground." (Luke 22:44).

We see other examples throughout the Gospels of Jesus praying intently before a major event. Early in His ministry, Jesus needed to decide which of the disciples would become the early leaders of His church. Luke tells us that Jesus "went out to the mountain to pray, spending the night in communion with God. At daybreak, he called his disciples and selected twelve of them to be his apostles." (Luke 6:12-13).

Think about that for a minute. Jesus spent the night in prayer. Jesus spent all night praying to His Father. Luke's passage conveys something else of significance, too. He says that Jesus was in communion with God. That tells us that Jesus' prayer with God was not a one-way prayer. It was a dialogue between Him and His Father. By being in communion with each other, He and His Father were one in prayer.

If Jesus needed to pray often – and Jesus was God – how much more important is it for us to pray frequently? Furthermore, it's natural to pray with a deeper intensity when we're facing a very challenging situation. We can be assured that God listens to our prayers. And, since in prayer we become one with God, we will feel God's peace. That peace will comfort us in our struggles, which itself is God answering our prayers.

October 5, 2023

GIVING GOD TROUBLE

We have another person who is always there for us - someone we can complain to, someone we can seek advice from, someone we actually can give our problems to, someone who we are assured loves us no matter what. We can give them to Jesus.

Have you ever had a day where nothing seemed to be going right? You wake up ready to face the day and start attacking your list of things to do. No sooner do your feet hit the floor than you receive a message from your child (not a phone call mind you, but a text message. Do kids ever make phone calls to their parents anymore?!). The car broke down on the way to school. So much for the to do list. Then, immediately after you fix the car problem, your uncle calls and asks you to drive him to a doctor's appointment. And it goes on from there.

Perhaps it happens during a long day at work. Your supervisor calls you into her office and berates you for a memorandum you spent all day writing that she found deficient. As soon as you arrive back at your desk, you get a call from your client demanding that you deliver immediately on a project for which they were two weeks late in providing the required information. It's one of those days that you just wish you could go home and get back under the covers. I've had many of them. We all have.

When experiencing such a day, it's really nice to have someone to commiserate with. My late wife bore more than her share of venting relating to my bad days. She was the best listener. And just knowing she loved me helped to make the problems less severe. Fortunately, I've recently been blessed to find Jessica, who similarly is a great listener and helps me work through the challenges life brings us.

I had a mentor at the firm who I could always call to blow off steam or go to for advice. It's rare that one person can do both, and I was lucky to have such a mentor.

During those difficult times, it's easy to forget that we have another person who is always there for us – someone we can complain to, someone we can seek advice from, someone we actually can give our problems to, someone who we are assured loves us no matter what. We can give them to Jesus. I facetiously refer to this as giving God trouble. But in fact, that's exactly what He wants! Jesus wants us to come to Him with all our burdens, worries and concerns. He wants us to come to Him as we are, not as we think He wants us to be.

There are many examples in the gospels of every-day people giving their problems to Jesus. The woman who was hemorrhaging certainly wasn't having a good day. In fact, she had experienced years of bad days. When Jesus appeared in her town, she didn't confront Him and complain about her circumstances and demand a change. She was too humble for that. Instead, she drew near to Jesus and simply touched his cloak. She gave her trouble to Jesus.

What was the result? Jesus gladly took her troubles and extinguished them. Jesus cured her immediately of her chronic illness. In fact, Jesus did more than that. He not only cured her ailment, He stopped and talked to her. He had compassion for her and forgave her sins, and in doing that Jesus saved her.

Talk about a complete transformation! The woman came to Jesus as she was and gave her troubles to Him. And Jesus changed her – physically, spiritually and emotionally. That no doubt made Jesus happy. You can almost picture Him smiling as he saw her reaction to her life being changed!

Maybe the next time we're having one of those bad days – and they will come – we can think of the woman in the Gospel story. Instead of spiraling into a negative frame of mind, we can stop and take a few breaths. Then, we can talk to Jesus and give our problems over to Him. He's waiting for us. He wants nothing more than for us to come to Him with all our problems. And when we do, He will smile as He comforts and helps us.

June 10, 2023

QUALITY TIME

One thing is for certain: Jesus will always make time for us, and He will never be preoccupied with past problems or future challenges. He is always in the present.

Quality time – we all long for it, especially time with our loved ones, be it our children or our spouse/partner. As I've gotten older, quality time has become more of a priority. I enjoy it when I get it, and I get frustrated when I don't.

After a long day at work, I would come home and look forward to catching up with my family over dinner, albeit often a late dinner because of my schedule. If the phone rang or I caught my son absorbed with his cell phone, I would get really annoyed. "Can't you put down your phone for five minutes?!" I would exclaim.

I similarly cherish quality time with my better half. And since I'm retired, I have an ample supply. However, Jessica has a job and kids at home, so her schedule is busy. Although I, of all people, should be able to relate, I have to remind myself to be patient and not be too demanding – to realize that she's doing the best she can.

It occurred to me that Jesus has the same problem with us. He longs to have a personal relationship with us. The way to develop a personal relationship with anyone is to spend quality time together. That's what Jesus wants with me – with us. He's constantly there, waiting.

What if I give the same priority to spending quality time with Jesus as I do with my son and Jessica? What if we all give Jesus the same amount of focus as we do the important people in our daily lives? The minute I realize that I'm going to be with my loved ones, I'm filled with excited anticipation. Is it the same in my relationship with Jesus? When a relative comes to visit, I immediately make time for them. Do I make time each day for Jesus? One thing is for certain: Jesus will always make time for us, and He will never be preoccupied with past problems or future challenges. He is always in the present. When we go to Him, He will never be distracted. He will listen, and He will guide.

It's quite ironic. I'm a structured guy. I think I have to do certain things to achieve certain goals – deliberate processes with defined steps. For example, to enhance my relationship with God the steps include doing more for others, being more charitable, etc. These action items are good and I should make time for them. I'm sure they please God. But the reality is Jesus wants time with me. He wants time with each of us. He wants us to talk to Him. He wants to communicate with us, to calm our fears, to share our joys. He wants quality time with us – no different than the quality time we want with the important people in our lives. Shouldn't Jesus be the most important person in our lives? Shouldn't we want to spend as much quality time with Him as possible?

The most incredible thing for us is that Jesus doesn't have high expectations. He died for us. If anyone deserves to have high expectations, it's Him. But He doesn't. He wants us to come to Him as we are, with all of our problems, our cares, our sins. He'll gladly take all of them, unconditionally. He just wants to be close to us. Let's make it a priority to spend quality time with Jesus each day.

March 13, 2023

GOD DOES NOT RATION THE SPIRIT

The more we ask for and utilize the Holy Spirit, the closer we will be to God, the source of all of our happiness.

As a child I often would read the Bible, particularly the Gospels. I read them as one does a book, for example, taking the Gospel of Mark and going in order. My older siblings teased me and called me a nerd because I was reading the Bible instead of other kid's books. In fact, I did read other books, too! I was a big fan of *The Lord of the Rings* and books of that genre. But I really enjoyed the Gospels. I obtained a different perspective by reading them chronologically as opposed to hearing various passages proclaimed each Sunday.

Recently I came across a spiritual reflection that encouraged people to spend 15 minutes each day reading the Bible. The suggestion brought back fond childhood memories. Back then I had the time to read the Bible each day. My situation is now similar given that I'm retired. I remembered how fulfilling it was, so I decided to resume the practice. There's no time like the present, so I started right away.

I picked the Gospel of John as my launching point. Before starting, I said a little prayer asking Jesus to fill me with His Holy Spirit as I read. I promised myself that I was going to read slowly and reflect on the words. I even told myself that, if it takes all fifteen minutes to read just one chapter, that's ok. With that, I began.

There's no question that I had a different experience. The words seemed to mean more, and I had a calm, relaxing experience. I really enjoyed it, just like I did when I was a kid.

In Chapter 3, I came across the following words from a discourse by John the Baptist: "For the One whom God has sent speaks the words of God; He does not ration his gift of the Holy Spirit." (John 3:34). I've been attempting to better understand the Holy Spirit, so these words really struck me – how incredibly powerful they are. God does not ration His gift of the Holy Spirit.

That means that the Holy Spirit is available to every one of us. We don't have to get in line for it. We don't have to make a reservation or get out our credit cards to make a payment. We don't have to pass a test. There's no group of people that get preferential treatment. It's a gift that God gives freely to all of us. We're all treated the same by God.

This passage also tells me that every one of us can have as much of this gift as we want. There's no limit. In fact, I'm quite sure that nothing would make God happier than if we asked for more of this gift. I really can't think of anything else in our lives that works this way.

The temporal things that make us happy are finite: a great vacation must come to an end; a delicious meal at a great restaurant will have a last course. But the gift of the Holy Spirit has no limit or ending. It's there whenever we want it and for as much as we desire. And the best part is that the more we ask for and utilize the Holy Spirit, the closer we will be to God, the source of all of our happiness. Think about it: The singular gift that can bring us true happiness is freely available to every one of us.

Even my small experience shows us how powerful the Holy Spirit is. I was inspired by the Spirit to resume reading the Gospel daily. I prayed to the Holy Spirit for guidance before I commenced. And I received this simple but amazing message about the Holy Spirit. As with so many elements of our faith, it's the ultimate virtuous circle.

We all have busy lives, and they seem to be getting busier. That's all the more reason to create a little downtime each day and read about the most fascinating and influential person in human history. It will be time well spent. In fact, I can't think of a better way to spend fifteen minutes of the day.

September 18, 2023

FAITH, HOPE AND LOVE

In order to have hope ⁃ hope in the spiritual sense ⁃ we need first to have faith. With that faith, we start to understand God's love. And it's God's infinite love that provides hope.

The past few days have been a rollercoaster of emotions. It's coming up on two years of being widowed and lately I've really started to feel the aloneness. I can deal with the fact that I'm going to be alone today, but it's more difficult to contemplate the future and the possibility of spending the next thirty years or so alone. That thought makes me sad. Each time it happens I turn to Jesus and talk to Him about it. And each time, I feel His comfort. That comfort comes from knowing Jesus will always be present with me, especially when I'm alone. However, it goes beyond that. He gives me a sense that He will help me to work things out. I don't know what His plan entails, but it's comforting to know that He's in control.

Earlier today, I watched via livestream the homily at St. Patrick's Cathedral in NYC. I don't usually do that when I've already attended Sunday Mass in person, but today I was inspired to do so. The priest commented that we are called to be a people of hope, not despair. That got me thinking. I certainly would say that my experiences with God over the past few days have characterized by hope.

In his epistle, St Paul talks of the virtues of faith, hope and love, the greatest of these being love. The Holy Spirit inspired me to reflect further on these virtues. In order to have hope – hope in the spiritual sense – we need first to have faith. With that faith, we start to understand God's love. And it's God's infinite love that provides hope. No matter what happens to us in our life on Earth, God loves us. If we remember that and love Him in return, we have everything. We have a true friend in Jesus who dwells within us and helps us to face any challenge because He faced the greatest hardship and triumphed. We also have a promise from God that we will go to Heaven when we pass from this life. That's hope.

Hope in God is a different concept than hope as defined by the secular world. Secular hope is something you wish for but have no ability to control ("I hope the Red Sox win their game today."). Hope in God is a confident hope; we're confident because we trust in God and His ability to provide. Because of our faith, we have come to understand God's love. In turn, the unending promise of that love gives us hope. It's very simple but profound. If we have this hope in God, it changes everything.

Bringing this back to what I've been experiencing the past few days, God's love gives me hope. When I'm feeling alone, yes, I should give that suffering up to God as a sacrifice in thanksgiving for what He has done for me. But there's more – much more. Whenever we're feeling alone, we need only remind ourselves that Jesus is with us. He's not even a phone call or text away. He dwells <u>inside</u> us. We merely need to talk to Him, and we will feel His presence. He's always there. He promised! "Behold, I am with you, even to the end of the age." That's love. And that is a reason to hope!

May 10, 2023 postscript:

In addition to being my companion in August of 2021 when I so needed Him, Jesus provided even more. Less than a month after I wrote the above reflection, I met someone in the most unlikely of ways. Over a short time, our friendship developed into a deep, loving relationship. That's yet another reason to hope and trust in God!

August 8, 2021

TEMPTATIONS

Just as it was necessary for Jesus to endure the temptations to be fully ready to carry out God's plan, perhaps the temptations we encounter in our lives help to prepare us to fulfill God's plan.

Today's Gospel reading (the first Sunday of Lent) describes the devil's temptations of Jesus after He had spent forty days in the desert preparing for His public ministry. The temptations were the final phase of the Lord's preparation. The humanity of Jesus was subject to these temptations. By resisting them and conforming to the will of the Father, Jesus completed His preparation. Jesus proved He was ready to proclaim the Word and to start His journey toward Calvary – the journey that would ultimately save all of us.

Listening to the Gospel today, I reflected on how this passage can apply to us. Just as it was necessary for Jesus to endure the temptations to be fully ready to carry out God's plan, perhaps the temptations we encounter in our lives help to prepare us to fulfill His plan for us.

God tested me prior to and after my late wife's death. As Jean's illness worsened, I prayed to God constantly that He would intervene and heal her. As I prayed, I had one hundred percent confidence that God would answer my prayers. I can't explain how, but I just knew it. I continued to believe that God would heal Jean even as her health further deteriorated. Right up to the day she died, I was convinced God would fully cure her. Needless to say, when Jean passed, I was shocked. I couldn't understand why Jean died, particularly given that, in my mind, God had told me He would heal her.

Over time I came to understand why God chose not to intervene – in short, because I believe God had other plans for Jean in Heaven. But today's Gospel may have provided some insight into how the course of these events impacted me. Given how shocked I was – I was certain God would heal her – I could have questioned my faith or maybe even rejected it. At times I thought about it. I definitely was confused. In short, I was tempted. For a time I felt like I was going through the motions at Mass and in my prayers. However, with the aid of the Holy Spirit, I didn't lose my faith.

In fact, over the course of those early months after Jean's death, I clung to my faith. Ultimately, with the Blessed Mother and others interceding for me, my faith became stronger and got me through a brutal period. While this was happening, God started to provide snippets of His plan for me.

With the benefit of hindsight, I realize that part of the reason God may have let me become so convinced that He would intervene was to test my faith – not for His benefit but for mine. My experience ultimately strengthened my faith in Him. As a result, I believe it made me more ready to start my ministry.

As is so often the case with God, good things can, and often do, come out of the difficult situations we face in our lives. We will always face temptations; that's just part of life. However, if we keep our trust in God, we will come out of those experiences stronger. During challenging times, our faith in God will be reinforced, and we will be more prepared to accomplish the ministry God has in mind for each of us. Once again, it comes back to faith, hope and love: faith in the love God has for each of us, and the resulting hope that our loving God will always be there when we most need Him.

March 6, 2022

BEING WITH GOD IN PRAYER

There are very few things in life we can say have no downside risk at all. Spending time with God is most definitely one of them.

Meditation and prayer are effective methods to spend time with God. Today, I meditated about prayer! The objective was to improve the quality of my prayer. If prayer is so important – and it no doubt is – how can I make my prayers better? Like most, when I pray I generally do one or more of the following: ask God for His help on certain things or for request healing for someone. Also, I recite certain prayers like the Rosary or a daily mini-novena to Mary.

While all these forms of prayer are okay, there is a common theme – the focus is on me and what I want. Even when I pray the Rosary, I'm almost often praying for a certain intention ("Mary, please intercede to help me with…"). It dawned on me that my prayer should be more about God and less about me and my needs. This is a very consistent message in books about prayer I've been reading lately. I also realized that it's important to spend more time each day in quiet reflection. While I'm sure God likes it when we talk to Him, He also wants us to slow everything down – bring our lives to a halt for even a few minutes and simply put ourselves into His Holy presence.

I've started to do this a little bit but need to get better – more disciplined in my approach and in the frequency. More often than not, nothing happens during this quiet time. I don't experience a locution from Jesus, although on occasion, Jesus does talk to me. I don't have visions. But any time spent with God is time well-spent. I suspect that, if I'm able to become more focused during the time I spend with Jesus, He will speak to me more frequently. No matter what happens or doesn't happen, the time I spend with Him is peaceful, incredibly peaceful.

There are very few things in life we can say have no downside risk at all. Spending time with God is most definitely one of them. If we try a little harder to make our prayer time more about God than about ourselves, we will experience quality time with Him, peaceful time. If we can be really quiet, attentive and patient, He will speak to us.

So where can we go to find a quiet place to be with God? A church is an obvious answer. After all, Jesus is present in the Tabernacle, and it's quiet. For many reasons, it may not always be possible to get to a church for meditation with God. Finding a comfortable spot at home with the electronics turned off generally works well for me. Alternatively, I've often experienced really effective prayer time while walking. It can be a little harder to clear the distractions (loud cars going by, etc.), but when I do, the results are amazing. I've had some of my best moments with Jesus when walking, particularly when I opened my mind to the signs of His presence all around me, be it the birds singing, the beautiful flowers or the waves breaking on the shore.

Finally, even when we're praying more actively (i.e., asking for something), we can still make it about God. If, after asking for our intention, we just remember to say a simple, "Thank you God" or "Jesus, I trust in you," we'll be making a small effort to make our prayer more about God and less about us. It's definitely a work in progress for me.

Thankfully, God is patient. He's always going to be there for us when we turn to Him. Why? Because, contrary to what we may do, God makes it about us and not about Him. We know that because He sent His Son to be sacrificed so that we could be saved and be with Him for eternity. So there is no better example we can look to than God for making not making it about ourselves. We'll never be disappointed in our prayer when we remember to put God first.

September 21, 2021

IN HIS VORTEX

Let the aura of His Spirit present in us, heal us, comfort us, strengthen us and give us peace.

Certain people project a larger-than-life persona. There's an aura surrounding them. We see it often in movie characters. The superhero who saves the day. It's the same with certain sports figures. The top athletes create a following wherever they go. People wait in line for hours just to catch a glimpse of their favorite star.

We see it occasionally in the business world as well. Many folks achieve success, but only rarely do we encounter an executive who simply commands a presence whenever he/she walks into a room. Everything stops and all attention turns to that person. I experienced this phenomenon with a few leaders during my career. My colleagues and I would often say, only half-jokingly, that we got pulled into his/her vortex. We wanted to be around them, hoping their aura would rub off on us.

What characteristics separate these people from the rest of us? There are no doubt many, but there are two traits common in all. Each one is exceptionally talented at his or her trade. It's almost as if they have supernatural abilities that the rest of us simply don't have. They can do things we can't seem to do. However, despite operating on another level, they're able to relate to those around them and make them feel special.

Jesus must have been like that for the Apostles. They lived with Him for three years and repeatedly saw Him do things no one else could do. He healed the sick. He cast out demons. He fed thousands. He raised the dead. He spoke with a wisdom that others could never approach. Yet, He was humble. He was of modest means, just like them. He had qualities that made them want to be close to Him. They wanted to be in His vortex. There was an aura about Jesus.

It wasn't just the Apostles who were drawn to Jesus. We read throughout the Gospels that large crowds followed Jesus wherever He went. People longed to hear Him speak. Some merely tried to touch His cloak in the hopes of being healed. The crowds were drawn into the vortex of Jesus. They were attracted to this humble man who possessed supernatural abilities. Many were so taken by Him that they misunderstood Jesus' mission and tried to make Him a king.

On the surface it may seem different for us than the crowds that followed Jesus. Jesus doesn't live with us in physical form. However, He does dwell within us through His Spirit. That means we actually can experience Him like the crowds did. We can feel His healing presence within us. We can let Him cast out the demons in our lives that keep us from Him. We can let His comforting words lift us up when we're feeling low. We can let His grace help us to be better Christians. We can spend some quiet time, emulate His humbleness and experience His peace. In sum, we can allow ourselves to be pulled into His vortex.

Unlike the super-athletes and leaders of our temporal world, there is a direct benefit for us when we allow ourselves to be pulled into Jesus' vortex. With Jesus, we don't just get a quick viewing or a brief introduction. No. We can experience His presence with us whenever we want it. The more time we spend with Jesus, the closer we'll become to Him. We will get pulled further and further into His vortex. To be close to Jesus means to experience His grace and to feel His peace.

Being in Jesus' vortex also means we will experience His cross. We will endure suffering. It's part of life, and it's part of being a Christian. It's not a bad thing. In fact, we shouldn't fear being absorbed into His cross. If we can better understand the extent of what Jesus did for us, we will benefit in two ways. First, a better awareness of the extent of the suffering He endured for our sake, will strengthen our faith in Him. How could it not? Secondly, we will be better able to deal with our own sufferings.

Today, let's allow ourselves to all be pulled into Jesus' vortex just like the crowds in His day. Let the aura of His Spirit present in us, heal us, comfort us, strengthen us and give us peace.

September 11, 2023

OUR CHRISTMAS GIFTS

The best way to ensure that we recognize God's gifts is to put God at the center of our thoughts, to pray for discernment and to take time to listen to Him.

There's something magical about New York City during the Christmas season. Yesterday, Jessica and I went to see Andrea Bocelli perform at Madison Square Garden. It was an exceptional experience. We rode the train from New Haven to Grand Central. We had a picnic dinner on the train. Once there, Jessica convinced me to take a pedicab to Madison Square Garden – an exhilarating but harrowing experience! God definitely was looking out for us as the driver swerved in and out of lanes between cars to get us to the concert quickly. But without question, the highlight of our trip was the concert.

I was familiar with Andrea Bocelli's music, but not enough to really appreciate it. All that changed last night. His voice is powerful yet beautiful; echoing yet soothing; all-encompassing yet paradoxically personal. At times I felt like he was singing just to me. He performed many songs with his two children, and the way he harmonized with them was mesmerizing. I don't think I've ever heard anyone sing more beautifully than Andrea. He and his family performed many Christmas songs, including several well-known religious ones. It was such a great way to get into the spirit of the season.

There is no doubt that God gave Andrea a special gift. Moreover, it became obvious to me during the show last night that Andrea is fully using the gift God gave him. With his physical handicap, Andrea would have had a very valid reason to say no to God. If it were me I might have said, "It's just going to be too hard to get on stage and perform in front of thousands of people." But Andrea did not. Instead, he overcame his handicap and embraced the gift God gave him. Consequently, he has brought joy to millions of people worldwide. In that regard, it could be said that Andrea is giving back to God in appreciation for the gift that God gave him.

I loved listening to Andrea perform, but the concert had a much more profound impact on me. The incredible beauty of his gift was a reminder to use the gifts God has given us to their fullest potential. Whatever gifts He has given me – given us – they're as important to God as the gift of song that He gave Andrea, and He desires us to use them.

In Andrea's case, the gift he was given was obvious. How could you not see the hand of God in such a beautiful voice? Sometimes, however, God's gifts are more subtle. That's more likely the case with our gifts. For instance, God's gift to one person may be the ability to listen to a family member who needs to talk out a problem. The best way to ensure that we recognize God's gifts is to put God at the center of our thoughts, to pray for discernment and to take time to listen to Him.

Several times during the concert I couldn't help but think that God must have been smiling as He listened to Andrea Bocelli making full use of the gift he had freely received from Him. It's the same with us. Every time we use our gifts, we are bringing happiness to others, and that makes God smile. We should think of it as our way of saying thank you to God.

We also should be thankful for the most important gift God gave us – His Son. Just like His other gifts, we didn't do anything to deserve it – quite the contrary, in fact. God freely gave us Jesus. God loves us so much that He wants us to be with Him, and the only way to ensure this was to send us His Son to suffer and die so that we could live.

Christmas is truly a wonderful season. It's a good time to remember to treasure the gifts God has given us and to thank Him for those gifts in the manner that makes God most happy – to use them each day. And as we're exchanging gifts with our loved ones, let's take a minute to remember the ultimate gift we have received from God – His Son.

December 15, 2022

THE MAGNET

When we turn our hearts toward Him, there is a magnetic pull. The closer we get to Him, the stronger the pull becomes. He wants us to feel the sensation of Him holding us in His arms, just like our moms did when we were kids.

I like to start each day by sending a text to my better half to let her know I'm thinking about her. Today I wrote the following: "Your heart is a magnet – it pulls mine toward yours, and it's getting stronger the longer we're together." Those words are absolutely true. I do feel my heart being pulled closer and closer to Jessica's.

Shortly after I sent the text, I went to daily Mass. As the priest held up the Host during the Consecration, the notion of a magnet popped up in my head again – this time in the context of Jesus pulling me toward the Eucharist. That same pull is there, not only in the Host, but in the Spirit of Jesus dwelling within us. The Spirit of Jesus dwelling in us is a magnet, drawing us toward His body in the Eucharist.

When I allow it to happen – when I put Jesus before everything else – I feel that pull. It may not be as strong as when the priest holds up the Eucharist, but it's there. He pulls all of us closer to Him, where we're safe because we're in His presence.

It's similar to the sense of security children have with their parents, especially their mothers. When I was a kid there were numerous incidents when I ran to my mom for security and consolation. One day I was playing football with my friends in the backyard. I tripped (not unusual for me!) and my knee hit a rock. I went straight to my mom, crying at the top of my lungs. She pulled me into her arms and told me everything was going to be OK. She promptly cleaned the wound and put a band-aid on it. It wasn't long before I forgot all about my mishap and was outside again playing with my friends. My mom always made things better. I always felt safe because of her.

Jesus provides that same feeling of security. He dwells within us. We can be assured that every time we go to Him with our problems, we will feel better. The problems may not go away, but we will feel better because He helps us deal with them. When I think about it, my mom didn't make my wound go away either. She helped me deal with it. Jesus does the same. When we turn our hearts toward Him, there is a magnetic pull. The closer we get to Him, the stronger the pull becomes. He wants us to feel the sensation of Him holding us in His arms, just like our moms did when we were kids. When we allow it to happen, we will feel the comfort of His security, but we also will feel an emotion even more profound. We will experience Christ's peace.

In the Gospel, Jesus, when speaking of peace, says, "Not as the world gives it, do I give you my peace." Is He ever right! When I experience His peace, there is a true serenity that overpowers everything else in my world – if even just for a few minutes. Today I experienced it twice – once during the moment at Mass, and the second time when I took a few minutes out of my day to sit quietly in His presence. What is most remarkable about these two experiences is that they occurred during a day that was busier than most for me. I never really stopped today. Yet those two moments were all that Jesus needed to be present with me.

So let us remember each day to let our hearts be drawn to the magnets in our lives – those special people whom Jesus has blessed us with and, more importantly, to Jesus Himself. We won't be disappointed.

May 11, 2022

HUMILITY

*Jesus, help me to remember today that it's not about me.
Please help me to put You first and to put
others before me.*

It's often said that pride is the worst sin. When I first heard the phrase I was confused. Wouldn't assault or murder be a more serious sin? However, as I reflected on it further, I realized that pride is in fact a terrible sin because we're putting ourselves ahead of God. And when we do that, bad things are going to happen. Sin begets sin.

Unfortunately, pride is insidious. I'm guessing that I put myself before God many times each day. It's insidious because most of the time I don't even realize that I'm doing it. Hopefully God is less upset with us when we don't do it intentionally. But still, it's a sin – we put ourselves first. Because pride is insidious and because we often don't realize what we're doing, it's used to maximum effect by satan, the ultimate insidious being.

It is also frequently said that humility is a virtue. Humility is the diametric opposite of pride. It's when we put God and others before ourselves. When we're putting God first, it's a lot harder to sin. I often find it helpful to think through things by using comparisons. The comparison here would be: If humility is the opposite of pride and pride is the worst sin, it must follow that humility is the greatest virtue.

At a very simple level, being humble is not difficult. I strive to be humble in my approach to life. I don't want people to think I'm arrogant, so I work hard to project the opposite impression. My aim is to be sincerely humble. But, if I'm being honest, I don't always succeed. On occasion, and generally in conversation with people that I don't know well, I have a tendency to feel pride in what I think I've accomplished. I also have a tendency to "rest on my laurels" with God when, in fact, I've done very little in service to Him.

It's absurd when I stop to think about it. Jesus made the ultimate sacrifice for us and is there for us whenever we need Him. Yet I have the audacity to sometimes feel like I'm doing enough for Him – e.g., "I went to Mass today, so that's good enough." To make matters worse, I tend to focus on my needs and not necessarily what God wants for me.

The solution is quite simple, and it's something I say every day as part of my morning prayers. Some time ago the Holy Spirit inspired me to write down several daily principles which should govern how I live each day. The first one is as follows: "Jesus, help me to remember today that it's not about me. Please help me to put You first and to put others before me." If I can just practice what I recite every day, I will be taking a big step toward making humility a reality in my life. Walk the talk.

Fortunately for us, we have a great guide who not only gave us instructions through His teaching, but more importantly, through the example of His life on earth. Jesus never dwelled on His own wants. He always had time for others. Even when He was tired and looking to rest, Jesus never turned down a person who came to Him in need.

Jesus was the all-powerful God. He cured people of their illnesses. He turned water into wine. He walked on water. If anyone could be proud, it was Jesus. After all, He was God. However, Jesus acted in just the opposite manner. He was humble and put others before Himself. His life was centered on God His Father, and all that He did for everyone emanated from that, resulting ultimately in Jesus giving His life so we could be saved. Jesus set the standard for humility. Jesus gave us a living example of the greatest virtue. It's up to us to decide whether to strive to follow that example.

We can't do it on our own, but we have the Holy Spirit to help us. When we let Him help us – when we put our trust in Him instead of ourselves – we'll know we've succeeded in being humble.

August 16, 2022

JESUS' TEARS

Jesus is heartbroken not for Himself but for each person who has rejected Him. His love is so strong for each of us that He is saddened when even just one of us turns away.

A few days ago I, like millions of others, grabbed all my favorite snacks and settled in to watch the Super Bowl. Sporting events can function as a release, where we get engrossed in the game and forget about the cares of our lives and the problems in the world. This year's contest certainly facilitated that, as the Eagles and Chiefs went back and forth throughout the game, with the outcome being decided in the last few seconds. I forgot about the real world for a few hours.

Unfortunately, reality reared its ugly head shortly afterward. During the broadcast of the game, I noticed a few commercials about Jesus. I found out later that they were sponsored by a nonprofit Christian group trying to spread the message of Jesus in our divided society. Boy, do we need His message!

However, I was dismayed to learn that the ads created an uproar on social media. Apparently, many people were offended by the ads. They posted that the ads were inappropriate and ruined their Super Bowl experience. I couldn't comprehend the venomous responses.

We all see commercials that don't appeal to us, but for

the vast majority, we don't post a public response describing our outrage. What prompted these folks to react so negatively? I don't know the answer, but I'm now convinced it's all the more important that we spread the message of Jesus. Our world needs Him more than ever.

I suppose that it should not come as a shock that there are people in our society who don't believe in Christ. It happened to Jesus during His public ministry. In the Gospel of John, it is written, "Despite his many signs performed in their presence, they refused to believe in him." (John 12:37). Imagine how saddened Jesus must have been by this. He had come down from Heaven to live among the people for the sole purpose of saving them, and many rejected Him. While He knew from the start what was going to happen to Him, He spent His time on earth encouraging people to repent and believe in Him. He gave freely but was rejected.

If the people in Jesus' time who lived among Him didn't believe, it's not surprising that there would be people in our society who would disregard Him as well. You can see the parallels. There is also another common thread: Jesus is just as saddened by those who don't believe in Him today as He was 2,000 years ago. It's not the typical sadness we would feel if someone rejected us – essentially feeling sorry for ourselves. No, Jesus is heartbroken not for Himself but for each person who has rejected Him. His love is so strong for each of us that He is saddened when even just one of us turns away. He wants all of us to live with Him forever no matter what our faults may be. We just have to say yes to Him.

That's true hope. And we need hope. We see so much in our world that points to people either forgetting about Christ or outright rejecting Him: the angry messages posted in response to the Super Bowl ads; people only thinking about themselves; the many acts of violence that we watch on the news day after day. All these acts sadden us, and they sadden Jesus. It's not what He came for. But He doesn't give up on us. He never will.

Jesus proclaimed, "I have come into the world as its light, to keep anyone who believes in me from remaining in the dark." (John 12:46). That's our source of hope. In a world where there is darkness, we can always look to Jesus. His light will help us navigate in the face of these challenges. He stands ready to forgive each of us for those times when we turn away from His light. Most importantly, His light illuminates the path for us to follow in our lives, the path that ultimately will lead us to be with Him forever, where there will be no more tears.

February 15, 2023

CHAOS

No amount of worrying is going to help us in chaotic situations, but trusting in God will. God knows what we're going through, and He knows what we need.

Have you ever been in a situation where you say to yourself, "This is just chaos!"? When I was young, my family would go to my grandparents for Christmas Eve dinner. My mom was one of nine daughters born to parents who had emigrated from Italy. The annual Christmas gathering was a huge affair, with aunts and uncles and cousins descending on my grandparents' house. There were multiple conversations happening simultaneously. I remember thinking that it was chaos! However, I'm sure my grandparents loved every single minute.

While it certainly was chaotic, I have very fond memories of those Christmas Eve celebrations. There have been other chaotic experiences that don't conjure up such pleasant memories.

The day before our sign-off on our annual audit was always a day of chaos. We were awaiting clearance memos from our teams around the world and trying to obtain them was like herding cats. In addition, we typically had numerous audit findings that we were still trying to resolve so we could issue the opinion. Everyone was running around trying to finish up. Each year there would be a moment when I wondered whether we would meet the filing deadline. Thankfully we always did, but the chaos of that final day was never fun.

We've all had those moments, whether in our work life or at home. Jesus had them too. The first time He preached to his neighbors in His hometown of Nazareth was one such instance. The townspeople were in the synagogue, and Jesus read them a passage from Isaiah. It was a prophecy about Himself. They should have been singing praises to God for bringing His son into their midst. Instead, Luke tells us, "At these words, the whole audience in the synagogue was filled with rage. They rose up and expelled him from the town, leading him to the brow of the hill on which it was built and intended to hurl him over the edge." (Luke 4:28-30).

Here was Jesus back in His hometown, and His former neighbors weren't very neighborly. In fact, they weren't nice at all. They forcefully dragged Him to a cliff and tried to throw Him off it. Certainly that was a chaotic time for Jesus. Jesus had many such instances of chaos, culminating with His Passion, where the word chaos would be an understatement.

It's instructive to reflect on how Jesus reacted in those times. He didn't panic. He didn't lash out at those around Him. He didn't lose His cool. No, Jesus had none of these responses, any of which would have been quite normal for us.

Instead, Jesus demonstrated two consistent traits. He stayed calm. And He trusted His Father.

When He was pushed to the edge of the cliff, His Father

freed Jesus from the arms of His foes, and Jesus calmly walked through the crowd to safety. During the Passion, Jesus remained calm and silent amid the beatings and the screams of the crowd. He obeyed the Father's will and submitted Himself for our sake. And His Father rewarded Him by raising Him on the third day.

When we're facing chaos, how do we react? The answer probably varies. Undoubtedly, our best bet would be to imitate Jesus – stay calm and trust in God. No amount of worrying is going to help us in chaotic situations, but trusting in God will. God knows what we're going through, and He knows what we need. After all, Jesus experienced chaos, the likes of which we never will encounter. With His Spirit dwelling in us, we have everything we need to deal with whatever situation we encounter in our lives.

Hopefully the chaos we experience will be like the happy memories from Christmas at my grandparents' house. We all can deal with those instances! But during those less pleasant times, putting our trust in Jesus and calmly moving forward will enable us to get through the storm every time.

July 15, 2024

DON'T FOLLOW THE CROWD

Are we really so different from the crowds at His trial?
Every time we turn away from Jesus, we reject Him.
Granted, we're not shouting, "Crucify Him!," but we are
signaling that we don't want Him.

"Crucify Him! Crucify Him!" The crowd shouted it over and over. The same people, who had bowed before Jesus as He entered Jerusalem just a few days earlier, now were calling for His death. What changed? Of course, we know that the Pharisees and Sanhedrin, afraid of losing their power, incited the crowd to turn against Jesus. And the people, being afraid of the leaders, complied.

Imagine how Jesus must have felt. He came to bring people back to God – to save them – and they were calling for His death. He had been abandoned by His closest friends and was being set up by the Sanhedrin. Now to top it off, everyone had turned against Him.

Several years ago I attended Good Friday service at a church in Lower Manhattan. During the reading of the Passion, when we play the part of the Crowd, we typically speak the words in a normal voice – a normal volume. At this service there was a choir in the loft at the back of the church. When the time came for us to utter the words, "Crucify Him!," the choir screamed at the top of their lungs. Their voices resonated through the church. I didn't expect it, and it was shocking. It was also haunting. And it put the Passion into perspective for me. That's exactly what Jesus experienced 2,000 years ago. The people in that crowd no doubt were screaming at the top of their lungs, calling for His death.

Jesus had endured a mockery of a trial and incurred an excruciating beating. He was in agony. Yet I'm guessing all of that didn't hurt Him as much as hearing hundreds of people screaming for His death – the people He came to save. In the face of this vitriol, Jesus didn't yell back. He didn't give them a nasty look. He didn't say to Himself, "I'll get them back in the next life." No. Jesus said and did nothing.

Instead, He willingly gave His life for them – and for us. In Matthew's Gospel, Jesus teaches that when someone harms us, we should not try to hurt them back, but rather turn the other cheek. That's what Jesus did during His Passion.

When reading the Passion I'm tempted to think, "I'm glad that I wasn't part of the crowd that rejected Jesus." Would we have been able to resist the urgings of the leaders and the peer pressure from our friends? I'm not sure I would want to know the answer in my case.

Are we really so different from the crowds at His trial? Every time we turn away from Jesus, we reject Him. Granted, we're not shouting, "Crucify Him!," but we are signaling that we don't want Him. Our actions are shouting a blunt message. And we no doubt hurt Jesus when we do, just like the crowd in His day. After all, He gave up everything for us too. He gave His life for us, only to be rejected again.

The reaction of the crowd led to Jesus' crucifixion. Pilate gave in because of them. If they weren't so belligerent, Pilate probably would have released Jesus.

It's easy to rationalize our behavior when others are doing the same thing. Everyone else is doing it, so I should too. This is a subtle and perverse form of peer pressure, and we have to focus intently on rooting it out when it creeps into our minds.

When we reject Jesus, it's not going to result in Him being crucified. Jesus already died for us. However, we don't want our actions to result in Him being separated from us. He will never abandon us, but we can abandon Him. The "crowd" in our world today is trying to pull us away from Jesus, from our faith. Let's be sure we don't follow the crowd, but instead follow Jesus.

June 14, 2024

NO ONE CAN TAKE IT AWAY FROM US

Their Messiah rose from the dead. Thus, their grief did become joy, just as Jesus had promised. And from that moment forward, no one could ever take that joy away from them.

Today's Gospel passage comes from the last discourse of Jesus. As they are about to leave the Upper Room and head to the Garden of Gethsemane, Jesus tells His Apostles, "You will weep and mourn, while the world rejoices; you will grieve, but your grief will become joy. I will see you again, and your hearts will rejoice, and no one will take your joy away from you." (John 16:20-22).

Although they didn't fully grasp the magnitude of what Jesus was telling them, the hearts of the Apostles were probably heavy as they left the room. Jesus had been talking about His Passion for some time by then, and now it must have been apparent that whatever He was predicting was about to take place.

In fact, in a few hours, the Apostles would grieve. Jesus, an innocent man and the one they had hitched their wagons to – their Messiah -- suffered immensely and died a horrible death. Their world caved in on them. As the Jewish leaders celebrated the death of Jesus, the Apostles mourned.

Yet Jesus' words were fulfilled. All of them. Three days after this cataclysmic event, an even more impactful event occurred: the most impactful event in all human history. Their Messiah rose from the dead. Thus, their grief did become joy, just as Jesus had promised. And from that moment forward, no one could ever take that joy away from them. Moreover, their joy became infectious. Today, hundreds of millions of Christians around the world are infected with the same joy. No one can take that joy away from us either.

Have you ever gone through an extremely difficult struggle? In the midst of it, you don't know how or even if you're going to make it to the other side. You're tempted to give up. But you don't. You persevere and, eventually, you prevail. An amazing feeling then comes over you. Partly, the emotion is relief, but it's also a feeling of immense satisfaction. You accomplished what you thought couldn't be done. And what do you say to yourself? "No one can ever take it away from me!"

Toward the end of my career, I was asked to lead the team for one of our firm's largest audit clients. I was excited but also apprehensive. It would be by far the biggest challenge of my career. I realized it was going to take a complete effort every single day. The client was massive, projected a global reach and engaged in all product offerings in its industry. What's more, I would be leading a team of several hundred people, based in New York and at locations around the world. Despite my apprehension I looked forward to it.

In fact, those five years were the most challenging of my

career. There were times when the road ahead seemed overwhelming. However, our team rose to the challenge. We overcame all obstacles. We worked extremely hard and persevered. We successfully signed off on the audit at the end of each year. When I finished my rotation on the client, I felt a tremendous sense of accomplishment, and I remember thinking, "I was the lead auditor for the one of the largest clients in the entire firm. No one can ever take that away from me."

Our faith journey works the same way. It won't always be easy, particularly in the world we live in today. On some days the challenges may seem overwhelming, just like they were for the Apostles. But Jesus will be right there with us the entire time, just as He was for the Apostles. If we don't give up – if we persevere – we will be rewarded. Jesus will be pleased with us, and we will feel Him smiling down on us. Most importantly, we will reach the ultimate milestone: eternal life in Heaven with Jesus. We then will experience the same joy the Apostles felt when they encountered the Risen Lord. And the best part? No one can ever take it away from us!

May 10, 2024

THINGS ARE NOT AS THEY SEEM

His followers thought everything was lost. On the contrary, at the very moment Jesus said, "It is finished," He had triumphed. He had achieved the ultimate triumph.

Do you ever find that things aren't as they seem? We form an opinion in our minds about something, and it's often difficult to change our perspective. Then reality hits us right in the face.

Several years ago I was assigned as the partner for a large audit client. It was a significant role for me, and I was a bit apprehensive about meeting my client contacts. In one of the first meetings, I found myself sitting across the conference table from a very imposing individual. He had a scowl on his face during the entire meeting, like he was mad at the world and didn't want to be there. My initial reaction was that this was not a nice guy, and I wasn't looking forward to having to work with him for the next several years – five years to be exact. I started to wonder what I had gotten myself into. He said nothing during the entire meeting, which, combined with his expression, made my impression of him get even worse.

After the meeting, to my surprise, he came up to me and

introduced himself and said that, if there was anything he could do help my transition to please let him know. He turned out to be one of most pleasant and helpful people I have ever worked with. He was very talented, respectful and thoughtful. He was proactive in bringing issues to my attention and genuinely sought my perspective. He was also humble, quick to give credit to those who worked for him. All in all, he was a great guy. And it turned it that scowl wasn't a scowl at all. It was just his natural expression. I learned a lot from that experience – in particular, to be careful not to pre-judge someone. I would have benefited from following the Lord's guidance to Samuel: "Not as man sees does God see, because man sees the appearance but the Lord looks into the heart." (1 Samuel 16:7).

If we stop to think about it, with Jesus things are often not as they seem. In fact, our conventional thinking often is turned upside down. In John's Gospel passage where Jesus cures the blind man (John 9:1-41), the Pharisees assumed the man was born blind because of some sin his parents had committed. Even after Jesus had cured the man and he told his story to the Pharisees, they refused to believe and they looked down on Jesus because He had performed the cure on the sabbath. They went so far as to throw the man out of the synagogue. In an ironic twist, it was not the man who was blind, but the Pharisees who were blind. They were not happy at all when Jesus pointed this out to them.

Of course, Jesus' Passion is the ultimate example of things not being as they seem. At the time of his most trying hour, His disciples had abandoned Him. Everyone, including the disciples, thought he had been defeated. After all, He had been mocked and beaten. He was forced to carry His own cross. He was nailed to that cross. When He uttered the words, "It is finished," and took His last breath, all His followers thought everything was lost. On the contrary, at the very moment Jesus said, "It is finished," He had triumphed. He had achieved the ultimate triumph. He had defeated the Jewish leaders. He had defeated satan. He had defeated death. It would take some time – three days – for His closest friends to realize it, but at precisely the moment where conventional wisdom said that He had lost, He actually had won – the greatest victory in the history of the world.

Being a follower of Jesus often requires us to suspend conventional thinking. He wants us to put our trust in Him when the cynicism of our world tells us not to trust anyone but ourselves. He asks us to put Him and others before ourselves. He will sometimes nudge us in a direction that we may not want to go, somewhere out of our comfort zone. We should trust Him. After all, He provided us with the best example of things not being as they seem: His death brought life.

March 20, 2023

NO PASSWORD REQUIRED

These gifts have been freely given by God, and they're available to each of us. The key to unlocking them isn't a unique password. It's simply a word: love...

In today's complicated world there are passwords for everything. We need a password to log onto our computers. A password is required to access our accounts, be they credit cards, bank accounts, investment accounts or utilities, just to name a few. We even need passwords to make online restaurant reservations or to log into our fantasy football leagues. While having some level of protection is good for sensitive information, like our bank accounts, I'm not sure I need a password for my fantasy football team. I don't think anyone would find my roster to be useful information!

The point is that pretty much everything we might want to access requires a password. From a security perspective that's a good thing. However, for some – certainly me – it also creates angst. I try to use different passwords for different sites, and consequently I have trouble remembering them. I also fret every time I receive a message that my password may have been compromised in a data leak.

Those messages seem to be all too common these days. Recently I received one: My username and password had been compromised. When I get such a message, I always worry about whether someone might have obtained the password to my bank account: Could someone be stealing all my savings? It's irrational and I try not to dwell on the thought, but it's difficult not to worry. When this particular message came, I had just finished my morning prayers. My thoughts immediately went the protection of my assets, but I was reminded by the Holy Spirit not to be so focused on worldly goods – or, better said, it's important to differentiate between the treasures of earth and the treasures of Heaven. While it's not a bad thing to have accumulated some savings, it is a bad thing to obsess over them.

A simple way to avoid this mindset is to continually remind ourselves that what we have here on earth came from the grace of God. It's not ours, and it's not coming with us when we pass from this world. On the other hand, the treasures of God – his unending mercy, the gift of His Son dwelling in us, His promise of eternal life, just to name a few – are freely given to us by God, and no one can take them away from us. We may give them up through our own actions, but no one can steal them. Unlike my bank account, no one can steal the password.

It's incredible when you stop to think about it: The most precious gifts we have can't be stolen by anyone. These gifts have been freely given by God, and they're available. The key to unlocking them isn't a unique password. It's simply a word: love – truly understanding God's love for us; our love for God, and our love for each other. That's all we need to share in the treasures of Heaven, and that love is freely accessible to every one of us. No password required.

September 22, 2021

"HOLD ON LOOSELY"

God is not asking us to give up everything and all our time to follow Him, at least not for most of us. What He is asking is that we not be so rigidly attached to our schedules that we're not willing to be flexible when He asks us to do something for Him.

"Hold on Loosely," a song by the rock group .38 Special, was one of my favorites when I was a kid. I loved the melody and the words – still do. The refrain is, "Hold on loosely, but don't let go. If you cling too tightly, you're going to lose control." The song came on the radio today and it occurred to me that, in fact, we do need to hold on loosely.

We need to hold on loosely to earthly matters, the things of the secular world, so that we can be open to what God wants. God most definitely has a plan for each of us, but He is not going to impose His will upon us. We must be open to listening for His voice, and we must be ready and willing to follow the path God has marked out for us.

We also need to hold on loosely to our plans. I am certainly one who likes to have a plan. Every day, I make a list of what I want to accomplish. If something or someone causes an interruption to those plans, I often get frustrated. Some of those interruptions might be an opportunity to connect with Jesus, but I'm afraid I frequently miss them because I'm not willing to change my schedule.

About a year ago I was in Maine visiting my mom who had just undergone a medical procedure. I was only planning on staying a few days. However, her recovery took longer than expected. My two sisters were in Maine as well (one of them lives there), and they encouraged me to stay longer. I had plenty of items on my "to-do" list, so I was ambivalent. Also, I had checked out of the hotel, and it was sold out. My sister had a quick solution for that – I could stay with her. Ultimately, I decided to stay. It was definitely the right decision. My mom enjoyed having us nearby as she recovered, and my sisters and I were able to spend quality time together – something we hadn't done probably since we were kids. It was a special experience. When I changed my schedule I thought I was doing something good for my mom, but in the end, I had benefited at least as much.

In the Gospels Jesus gives us an example to follow. In Luke, Chapter 19, Jesus is passing through Jericho. He's not planning to stop there. However, He sees Zacchaeus in the sycamore tree and is moved with compassion. He changes His schedule and decides to have dinner with Zacchaeus. Jesus' flexibility changes Zacchaeus' life. In fact, it saves him.

This concept of being flexible with our time and the other gifts God has given can be difficult. I like to manage my own schedule, especially now that I'm retired. The good news is God is not asking us to give up everything and all our time to follow Him, at least not for most of us. What He _is_ asking is that we not be so rigidly attached to our schedules that we're not willing to be flexible when He asks us to do something for Him.

It comes back to the simple saying: everything in its proper order – with God being first. If, in fact, God is asking us to give up something we really like, we should trust Him. God will never ask us to sacrifice if He doesn't have something else even better in mind for us. In the book, *In the School of the Holy Spirit*, Jacques Philippe wrote, "We cannot receive the motions of the Holy Spirit if we are rigidly attached to our possessions, our ideas, our point of view." (p. 35). So, "Hold on loosely!" But hold on tightly to the hand of God.

May 16, 2023

SEE THE BALL

When we get distracted during prayer, we should remember to visualize where we're going. Thanks to God's love for us, we're on the path to Heaven.

When I retired I took up golf. I had played very little golf up to that point, and I was determined to become a good player. Three-plus years later, that still hasn't happened. I could make all sorts of excuses – I haven't played enough; I need to take more lessons; I should go to the driving range several times a week. Each of these statements is true. However, none of them get at the root cause. The root cause is simple to detect but harder to fix. It's in my head.

I overthink every aspect of the game. Are my feet positioned correctly? Am I using the right club? What about the water on the right side of the fairway? And forget about any chance of success if I'm paired up with someone, especially if they're good. At that point, all my mind can focus on is what will go wrong with my next swing and what their reaction will be.

Recently, when lamenting my consistently poor play, I received sound advice. I was told to visualize my shot before I started my swing. Look out to fairway and see where I want the ball to land. Then, visualize the shot and the ball landing in that exact spot. See the ball. It seemed simple, almost too simple. But I had nothing to lose, so tried it the next time I played. To my immense surprise, it worked! I won't claim that I hit the ball exactly where I had envisioned, but it was close. Visualizing where I wanted to hit the ball eliminated the distractions from my mind, and I focused on the swing.

There's another aspect of my life where I have a tendency to lose my concentration -- to get distracted. It's a much more important aspect of life than golf: my spiritual life.

Too often when I'm praying, I start thinking about something else, and it's completely unrelated to my prayer. It might make sense if I were praying for a relative to recover from an illness and my thoughts wandered to that relative. However, that's not typically the case. More frequently my mind goes to silly things: When am I going to get to the grocery store? Do I have time for the gym today? I had chicken for dinner last night; what am I going to have tonight?

It's crazy – these are such silly distractions to have during a time as important as prayer. It even happens during Mass. In fact, sometimes it's worse during Mass.

What's the solution to this problem? I'm not sure, but today I had a thought. It came during Sunday Mass when, not surprisingly, I was distracted. What if the solution for prayer is the same as for golf: to visualize where I want to be with my faith, where I want my spiritual journey to take me and how I'm going to get there.

We can push the distractions out of our minds by visualizing what our faith journey should look like. We can reflect on the events in Christ's life as documented in the

Gospels. In particular, we can meditate on His suffering and death and what He accomplished for each of us.

We can envision how we can reach out to help a relative in need today – with something as simple as a phone call, or perhaps bringing them something they love from the local bakery. Instead of the needless distractions, our minds can turn to our faith journey: envision the goal and how we're going to accomplish it. See the ball.

The golf analogy may have popped into my head from a show I watched before Mass. A commentator was observing a golf pro – one of the best in the world – as he took practice shots. The golfer informed the commentator that he visualizes every shot before he starts his swing. It was the same advice I had been given, and particularly impactful. It turns out even the best in the world envision their shots. His comment may have been the inspiration for my thought during church. Or perhaps it was the Holy Spirit speaking to me. Maybe it was a combination of both.

Regardless, the golf analogy resonates. As we pray, we should keep our focus on God. He loves us with boundless mercy. He sent His only Son to suffer, die and rise, so that we could be freed from our sins and spend eternity with Him. We pray to worship Him, to thank Him for His incredible mercy. We pray for loved ones. We also pray for ourselves – maybe too much.

We would do well to be more mindful of God's incredible mercy and make thankfulness a more prominent part of our prayer. And when we get distracted during prayer, we should remember to visualize where we're going. Thanks to God's love for us, we're on the path to Heaven. Our inheritance was purchased by the sacrifice of

Jesus, and that inheritance is eternal happiness in Heaven. Focusing on our inheritance will expel the distracting thoughts when we pray. See the ball. See eternal life with Jesus.

March 16, 2024

WINNING

When we turn to Jesus and let Him coach us, we win. Always.

There's a series on HBO called *Hard Knocks*. Each season it chronicles the experiences of the players and coaches on a professional football team as they go through training camp. I was watching an episode a few days ago in which the head coach and several players were discussing the concept of winning. They described the feeling associated with winning a game, and to a person they commented that there is no better feeling than winning. That may be a bit of a stretch, but we all can attest to the fact that it feels good to win – even if it's just in a game of cards.

Winning a game is fun, but it's not important in the grand scheme of things. Where winning becomes important is in our life's journey. Specifically, if we believe in Jesus and follow His teachings, we will win because He has already secured the ultimate victory for us. As we do our best to follow Jesus and live a Christian life, the world throws a lot of obstacles in our way. Sometimes things get so difficult, we might just want to give up. I know I certainly felt that way at times over the past few years while I was dealing with the loss of Jean. But Jesus pleads with us to never give up. He was with me, encouraging me, nudging me closer to Him, so He could help. Somehow – actually, I know how—I got through it. Every football team will have a difficult game in which everything seems to be going wrong. In response the players have to rally each other to persevere and prevail. Similarly, we will have tough days. When we do, we must remember to turn to Jesus. With His help we will rally, persevere and prevail.

Sarah Young writes as follows (in the voice of Jesus): "When you're in the thick of battle, declare your trust in Me… Hold tightly to My hand, and just keep standing. This is victory." (*Jesus Always*, p. 253).

When we turn to Jesus and let Him coach us, we win. Always. We win the daily challenges of life because He is at our side, reminding us of what's really important. We prevail against the most difficult tragedies because His Holy Spirit is within us giving us the strength we need and never knew we had. Finally, we gain the ultimate victory – eternal happiness in Heaven when our journey here on earth comes to its end. Yes, there is no better feeling than winning – winning with Christ.

August 30, 2022

MOVING FORWARD

If we don't continue to make progress, Christianity will stagnate. Our personal faith will stagnate. It's up to each of us to generate that forward momentum.

"If you're not moving forward, you're moving backward." I'm not sure who coined this phrase, but I use it often in my own life. It was this attitude that got me through the absolute devastation I felt after Jean passed away. Despite feeling immense grief, I pushed myself to make forward progress, even if it was just a tiny step at a time.

Similarly, during my work days, there would be times when the to-do list seemed overwhelming. That typically was the case when we approached the end of the annual audit. There were too many tasks to get done and not enough hours in the day to do them.

It's easy during those periods to simply freeze up. What's important is to just start "doing." Even completing one small task is progress. An item can be checked off the to-do list. It starts to build momentum, perhaps a very small amount at first. But that momentum is forward progress. Before too long, more items have been checked off, and the light at the end of the tunnel no longer feels like an oncoming train.

Achieving forward progress in the face of a daunting challenge also helps make you feel better mentally. Forward momentum leads to a positive attitude and can quickly generate a virtuous circle. The results can be amazing.

The early leaders of the Church faced a ton of adversity. They were persecuted by the Jews and the Gentiles alike. Thankfully, they didn't freeze up. They persevered, and they moved forward. It very well may have seemed like slow progress to them, but it was progress nonetheless. They looked forward, not backward. Their positive attitude and effort helped to spawn Christianity. Because of the efforts of a small group of people, over two billion of us today refer to ourselves as Christians. If the early disciples hadn't pushed forward, Christianity would have receded, and the efforts of Jesus would have been in vain.

It's the same today. If we don't continue to make progress, Christianity will stagnate. Our personal faith will stagnate. It's up to each of us to generate that forward momentum. With all of the challenges we face as Christians today, it can be easy to freeze up, not knowing what to do. Similarly, many may adopt an attitude of indifference, thinking what can I do that will make any difference at all?

This is not forward progress. And if we're not moving forward, we're moving backward.

So what can we do? We can begin small. For starters, we can spend just a few more minutes each day in prayer with Jesus. Time with Him will help to put us in the right frame of mind and will enable us to be receptive to His guidance. We can spend more time reading Scripture and reflecting on the Word of Christ. We can make that phone call to a relative who lives alone and would love to have someone to talk to for a few minutes.

These are little things that won't take up much time at all. But these little things represent progress – forward movement.

Each little task that my team and I checked off our list inched us closer to the end of the audit. While we were in the heat of battle, it was difficult to see progress. But we knew we were moving forward, approaching the finish line. And with every passing day, our positive momentum grew. The energy was palpable as I walked through the audit room.

We can generate that same energy with our spiritual life. If we strive to make progress every day the momentum will build on itself. It will feel good, and we will want to do more. Our energy will radiate out to those around us. That's how we can positively impact Christianity.

It's true that if you're not moving forward, you're moving backward. It's also true that forward movement, even if it starts small, can have an overwhelmingly positive impact. It can fundamentally change not only us, but the lives of those around us. The results truly can be amazing.

July 25, 2024

LOOK UP

Seeking the face of Jesus gives us much more. It compels us to look forward, not backward. It prompts us to look up, not down.

Have you ever gotten into one of those proverbial "funks?" I'm guessing we've all had them. We keep looking back on something we either did or did not do and we can't stop thinking about it. Quite often, it's a rather trivial matter, but that doesn't prevent us from obsessing over it.

I had one such experience almost four years ago, and I still think about it. It involved my late wife, Jean. It surfaced again today, perhaps because today is our wedding anniversary. It was a warm night in June of 2019. Jean was battling an insidious disease. She never gave up, and she never lost her positive spirit. As we were going to bed, Jean asked me if I would go downstairs and get her some fresh watermelon for a little late-night snack. It was a really minor request, but it was late, and I had set my alarm for 4:30 a.m. because of an early meeting in New York City.

Instead of going to get it, as she would have done for me, I responded, "It's late and I'm tired. Can't you wait until breakfast?" Of course, Jean was fine with that. She never complained. As it turned out, Jean's health took a very significant downturn two days later and I never had a chance to give her the watermelon. The memory haunted me for months afterward and still pops into my head occasionally.

I didn't act like a Christian that night. And while I'm sure that God wasn't happy with me, He also would not have wanted me to keep looking back. He wants us to learn from our mistakes but not obsess over them.

We often hear the phrase "seek His face." With every passing day I'm growing to love that phrase more and more. It conjures up a beautiful image. It evokes a feeling of peace. How can we not feel serene and calm when we're thinking of Jesus? Those are all good things. But seeking the face of Jesus gives us much more.

It compels us to look forward, not backward. It prompts us to look up, not down. We would never look down in search of God. We always look up for God. After all, God is in Heaven, and like little kids, we tend to look up when we're seeking Heaven. And by looking forward – to Jesus – our outlook is transformed. Instead of wallowing in the past, we pull ourselves up and move forward. Our hope is restored, and that changes everything.

It was difficult for me to look forward in the months after Jean passed. I simply couldn't get out of my funk. But Jesus never left me, and He pulled me toward Him. Today, when that memory came back, I was sad for a moment, but then I remembered to seek His face. When I did, He changed my channel. I was reoriented, looking forward. And I was reassured in knowing that Jean has an unlimited supply of watermelon in Heaven!

Seek His face, and never abandon hope – hope in Jesus.

April 13, 2023

THE ANSWER KEY

If we turn to Jesus and follow His teachings in the Gospel, we always will know what the correct answer is.

In my college days I typically would get stressed before upcoming tests. The bigger the test, the more stress I experienced. The stress peaked during final exam week, when the test would cover the syllabus for the entire semester.

Every once in a while, the teacher would throw us a bone. On those rare occasions the professor would announce, "Next week's exam will be an open book test," and the entire class would cheer. All the stress would vanish because the answers to the questions would be right in front of us – in the book on our desk.

Incredibly, the most important test we'll ever take during our lives is an open book test. Actually, it's one step better: We've been given the answer key! For our spiritual journey, our goal is to attain Heaven when we pass from this world. Thanks to our merciful Father, we know exactly what we need to do reach this goal. God sent His Son to show us the way to Heaven. The Gospel writers captured Jesus' teachings, so we all can study and benefit from them. Finally, if that weren't enough, God then sent Jesus to dwell in each of us through the Holy Spirit.

Is being a Christian difficult at times? No doubt the answer is yes. However, regardless of how hard our situation may be, we know exactly what we need to do to persevere in spite of the challenges we face. Jesus tells us to believe in Him and to trust in Him. When we do that – when we turn to His Holy Spirit – we will have both the strength and guidance we need. And we will be on the path to Heaven.

In our secular lives, we also will face difficulties. For example, in school we may be given a really tough math problem. We may not know the answer, and all we can do is work hard to try and figure it out. At our jobs, we similarly may encounter a seemingly unsolvable issue. At my accounting firm, I occasionally faced a client query where there was no clear answer in the literature. In response, I worked tirelessly with my team to determine the best solution. In these situations, we didn't always know whether we had gotten to the correct answer.

That's not the case with our spiritual lives and the resultant challenges we encounter. If we turn to Jesus and follow His teachings in the Gospel, we always will know what the correct answer is. It's a prime illustration of how God helps us to become good Christians. Not only does He give us the answer key, He also provides direct assistance. He has given us the gift of His Son dwelling in us. It's not an exaggeration to state the God has stacked the deck in our favor to help us return to Him.

When you stop to think about it, God must really, really love us and must really want us to be with Him for eternity if He's willing to give us the grace and strength we need to follow the simple instructions He laid out for us. Despite the fact that we're all sinners and inevitably turn away from Him at times, He wants us back.

All we have to do is say "yes" to God, and He will take care of the rest. And even after that, He still helps. I certainly am living proof of that. There is no doubt that God reached out to me, and gently but persistently, nudged me toward Him, not the other way around. I'm just beginning to understand the depth of the love God has for me, and that it's a very personal love. He desires that His Son dwell within us and actually befriend us! Furthermore, He wants that friendship to continue forever in Heaven. That's why He gave me – and all of us – the answer key.

February 17, 2024

OUR SECRET WEAPON

We, too, possess that same secret weapon. The Holy Spirit dwells within each of us and enables us to do extraordinary things.

When I was a kid one of my favorite television shows was the *Six Million Dollar Man*. It was a show about a man who could perform superhuman feats. He could run faster than a car. He could lift incredibly heavy things. He was far stronger than any other person. Yet he didn't look particularly fast or strong. In fact, he looked like any other person. However, he had a secret weapon. He had bionic arms and legs, and they enabled him to do things that no other human being could do.

I think we can view the Holy Spirit as a secret weapon that gave the Apostles supernatural strength. They had spent three years with Jesus, but they didn't fully comprehend who He was. Even after Jesus died, rose from the dead and appeared to the Apostles multiple times, they still didn't fully grasp what had happened. What's more, they lacked the courage to speak about it.

That is, until they received the Holy Spirit on Pentecost. That changed everything. The Holy Spirit filled them with the wisdom to finally understand the enormity of who Jesus was and what He had done. And with the Holy Spirit dwelling within them, they became fearless. Armed with the Holy Spirit, they boldly proclaimed what they had been witnesses to and preached a message of repentance. Their courage got the Church off the ground. They did things they previously couldn't do. They performed miracles. They became leaders of the Church. They were given strong powers – a secret weapon. That secret weapon was the Holy Spirit.

We, too, possess that same secret weapon. The Holy Spirit dwells within each of us and enables us to do extraordinary things. Maybe we're not going to perform physical miracles, but we can draw strength from Him to perform acts that we otherwise couldn't or wouldn't have been able to do. They may be simple acts, but they can have supernatural effects. For example, we might take some time out of our day to call a family member who we know is down in the dumps. It may not seem like much to us, but that call just might turn that person's day around. We can make a difference if we let the Holy Spirit inspire us, and we act on it. Perhaps we know of an elderly neighbor who would love to attend Mass, but cannot because they no longer drive. We could offer to give them a ride. That's the Holy Spirit at work within us.

We can look to the Holy Spirit to guide our thoughts and help us to act as God would want us to do. When we do so, in our own way, we're acting like the Apostles. We can make a difference in the lives of others not only by what we do for them, but also by the example we set. We can accomplish feats that we otherwise couldn't. In our own way, we can become leaders for our church.

Often, I'm underwhelmed by my sense of what I can do.

In other words, I wonder how whatever little thing I might do will have an impact in the grander scheme of things. What difference can I really make? When I think this way, I end up doing nothing. t's easy to get trapped in this loop.

When we read about the Apostles and the early Church in Acts, they were preaching to large crowds, healing people and standing up to the Pharisees. We look at them as larger-than-life figures. And they were. But, very probably, the reality was that they started small. When they first left the upper room, they may have encountered a few people as they were walking and perhaps started to talk to them about Jesus. Maybe those folks brought them to their homes for dinner, and they spoke to a few more people. The point is that, even though they were inspired by the Holy Spirit, it may have taken a little time for them to become the early leaders of the Church. But God had a plan for them, and they carried it out according to His will.

God has a plan for us, too. And, like the Apostles, we are inspired by the Holy Spirit. We don't have to change the world overnight. We merely need to trust God and do our best to carry out His plan. I heard a great line recently: No one can do everything, but everyone can do something. That's true – even more so when we use our secret weapon.

April 5, 2023

PAUL E. TUPPER

OH COME, LET US ADORE HIM

Jesus is our light – all the time. When we understand that, when we truly believe it, the darkness cannot overcome us.

It's the most joyous day of the year. We prepare for weeks, decorating our houses, shopping for presents and traveling to visit family and friends. As Christmas day approaches, our anticipation builds. When we were kids, we couldn't wait to open presents and start playing with our new toys. As adults we are also excited: We share in the thrill of the younger ones as they open their gifts. If I'm being honest, I also look forward to tearing off the wrapping paper to see what Jessica and my son got me! As the song goes, "It's the most wonderful day of the year."

Of course, there's a reason for the celebrations and presents – the ultimate gift to each one of us: the birth of our Savior. It's a bit ironic. When Jesus was born almost no one was aware of this event that changed the course of history. No one exchanged gifts; no hymns sung in the churches. There wasn't even a cradle to lay the baby Jesus in. The only people in the loop were some local shepherds who were told of His birth by the angels. When the shepherds heard the news, they went to the stable. They went there to worship the newborn King.

Every year, we go to worship too. We dress up in our finest clothes and go to celebrate the birth of our Savior and King. It's the one time of year that I think everyone in the church sings along to the hymns. No one is silent. When the entire congregation sings, "O come, let us adore Him," it's a magical moment. It certainly was for me today. There was a full orchestra, a pipe organ and a choir that sounded like it was comprised of professional singers. As we sang along with them, I felt like our words were reaching all the way to Heaven. And that's how it should be – not just on Christmas day, but every day of the year. O come, let us adore Him.

The Gospel reading for the Christmas Mass was taken from John. "In the beginning was the Word; the Word was in God's presence, and the Word was God. He was present to God in the beginning. Through him, all things came into being, and apart from him nothing came to be. Whatever came to be in him, found life, life for the light of men. The light shines on in darkness, a darkness that did not overcome it." (John 1: 1-5).

Jesus is the light, and the darkness has not overcome it. The darkness will never overcome it. As long as we don't let it.

We've all had times of darkness in our lives, times when it's really difficult to see the light. When my wife passed away, everything seemed lost to me. It felt like my heart had been ripped out of me. Nothing in my life felt right. It was as if a shadow was cast over everything, not only emotionally but physically as well. But ultimately, His light prevailed.

Jesus remained with me – within me – and eventually I came out of my fog. Jesus is the light, and the darkness cannot overcome it.

Jesus is our light – all the time. When we understand that, when we truly believe it, the darkness cannot overcome us. The only way the darkness can ever prevail is if we allow it to do so – if we give up and stop trusting in Jesus. As long as we maintain our hope in Christ and keep our gaze fixed on Him, we will live in His light.

That, for me, is the meaning of Christmas. Jesus was born in the middle of the night – in the darkness. Jesus is light and His birth dispelled the darkness. Christ lives in us today through His Holy Spirit. Through that Spirit, He is always with us. He is our light, and all the darkness in our world can never block that light unless we refuse to believe. We must never let that happen.

Two-thousand years ago, the shepherds and the angels sang joyful words. Today, we sing the same words. We sing them because our Savior dwells among us. He is the light, and the darkness cannot overcome it. The light of Jesus radiates joy and inspires hope.

O come, let us adore Him! Let us adore Jesus our light every day of our lives.

Christmas 2024

ABOUT THE AUTHOR

Paul E. Tupper was born and raised in Connecticut, the youngest of four children. He grew up in a faith-filled family: His father, Paul, was a Deacon in the Church, and his mother, Aurora, was the Head of Religious Education for their parish for many years.

Paul graduated from the College of the Holy Cross with a degree in Political Science, and subsequently earned a Master's in Accounting from Northeastern University. Paul then took a job with a public accounting firm in their audit practice. He spent his entire career, spanning thirty-four years, with that firm, mostly in their New York City office.

After retiring in late 2020, Paul commenced writing. Initially, it was mostly journaling as he started to better comprehend his faith. Over time, in response to a calling from God, the journal entries evolved into short reflections. The reflections typically included anecdotal stories coupled with spiritual messages that, in effect, chronicled his faith journey.

In addition to writing, Paul's interests include reading history, listening to classic rock music and learning to play golf. Above all, Paul loves spending time with his family: his son, Paul Joseph, and Jessica and her children.

He resides in Florida and New York.

www.ingramcontent.com/pod-product-compliance
Lightning Source LLC
Chambersburg PA
CBHW071301110426
42743CB00042B/1128